GURDJIEFF

A VERY GREAT ENIGMA

#45220 Highsmith Inc. 1-800-558-2110

GURDJIEFF
A Very Great Enigma

J.G. Bennett

SAMUEL WEISER, INC.

York Beach, Maine

First published in 1973 by
Samuel Weiser, Inc.
Box 612
York Beach, Maine 03910-0612

This revised edition published in 1984

99 98 97 96 95 94
9 8 7 6 5 4 3

Library of Congress Catalog Card Number: 83-50422

ISBN 0-87728-581-0
MG

Cover photograph: G. I. Gurdjieff in New York,
January, 1924

Printed in the United States of America

The paper used in this publication meets the minimum re-
quirements of the American National Standard for Perma-
nence of Paper for Printed Library Materials Z39.48-1984.

CONTENTS

GURDJIEFF'S BACKGROUND

Gurdjieff was a very great enigma in more ways than one. First and most obvious is the fact that no two people who knew him would agree as to who and what he was. If you look at the various books that have been written about Gurdjieff and if you look at his own writings, you will find that no two pictures are the same. Everyone who knew him, upon reading what other people have written about him, feels that they have not got it right. Each one of us believes we saw something that other people did not see. This is no doubt true. It went with the peculiar habit he had of hiding himself, of appearing to be something other than he really was. This was very confusing, and it began from the time he was first known in European countries.

Another enigma connected with Gurdjieff, concerns the sources of his teaching and methods. He never openly disclosed where he himself had learned. Anyone who takes the trouble to examine his teaching and his methods, can assign nearly every fragment to some known tradition. We can say that this theme came from the Greek Orthodox tradition, that theme came from an Assyrian or Babylonian tradition, another was clearly Muslim and connected with Sufism and even with this or that particular Sufi sect. One can say of others that they must have come from one or other of the branches of Buddhism. Again, there are indications that he took much from what is called the Western occult tradition, the Platonic and Rosicrucian tradition. But when one examines still more closely, we find that there is something that cannot be assigned to any known traditions. There are certain very important features of which one cannot find any trace in literature. I will have more to say about these in the next lecture.

If Gurdjieff were no more than a syncretist, a reformer who put together fragments from various well-known traditions or even secret traditions that he managed to unearth in the course of his search, then he would occupy one place. If, on the other hand, there is something wholly original, which cannot be referred back to any earlier known or secret tradition, then he occupies quite a different place. Herein lies the second enigma of Gurdjieff; which of these two places does he occupy? Was he just a clever man who was able to travel and search widely, to discover many things, to read a great deal, having access to sources in many different languages, and out of all the material so collected, to construct something? Or, was he a man who, in addition to all that—because he certainly did all that—had some direct insight that was peculiarly his own, and that was both important and also not traceable to any earlier source? That would make him a man of special importance, because true innovators are very rare in the history of spiritual ideas.

There is a third enigma about which I am going to speak specially this evening because it struck me with great force, when I visited the scenes of

Gurdjieff's early days a few weeks ago; and that is to explain how such a man could have come from such an environment. I saw, playing in the town of Kars in what used to be the old Greek Quarter, scores of little boys who ran after us wanting to be photographed and asking for bakshish: any one of whom might have been a young Gurdjieff. But the highest any of those boys can aspire to is probably to become a chauffeur, or possibly to get into the police —which is also a coveted profession.

The region between the Caucasus and Kurdistan is a very strange part of the world, and I must start by telling you a little about its geography and history. I had this map made, and it is an arrangement of the maps of this part of the world with which you are probably not familiar; as the usual maps tend to show Turkey in Asia, Russia, and Iran as separate units. In reality, this region is a coherent and well-defined geographical unit. (See Map of the Near East shown on page 4.) It is well-defined because it is dominated by the great mountains of the Caucasus and Kurdistan, with Mount Ararat here, the highest mountain after you leave the great central Asian massif right away until you come to the Mediterranean. Ararat is higher than any of the mountains of the Alps. These great mountain areas cover a greater surface than the Alps. Most of the area on this map is more than 3,000 feet above sea level, and the highest mountains go up to 15,000 feet and more. There is a great natural barrier that separates Europe and Asia. It runs from the Urals in the North, through the Caspian Sea to the great masses of the Caucasus and Kurdistan shown on the map. This barrier has checked the migrations of popula-

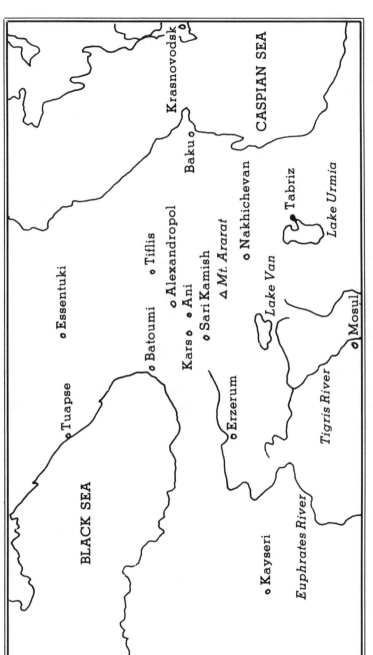

GURDJIEFF'S HOMELAND

tions east and west except through a few narrow channels. The most important of these channels runs northwest from Tabriz to Kars and then almost due west through Erzerum where it joins the valley of the Euphrates River. To the east of Erzerum is a watershed at a height of about 7,000 feet above sea level; but the pass can easily be negotiated in summer.

From time immemorial, and by that I mean a good 10,000 years, people have passed through that route. After the ending of the Ice Ages, when people began to travel southward and occupy these regions, this was one of the great migration routes. Wave after wave of invasion has entered that way: Parthians, Karduks and Armenians, Tartars, Mongols, and Turks. Genghis Khan and Tamerlane and other famous conquerors followed this route. The Seljuks and Ottoman Turks between the 10th and 15th centuries established Islam in Asia Minor by the way of the Caucasus route. Each wave of invasion was resisted, and one of the natural places of defence against invaders was a natural fortress that for many centuries has been known as the Fortress of Kars. When one stands upon Kars fortress, built on a rock dominating a narrow valley, one sees mountains in every direction, covered with snow at all times in the year. Kars has been besieged, defended and taken, again and again. At one time, it has been not Kars itself but the nearby city of Ani, which was the capital of the Bagratian Armenian kingdom of the 8th and 10th centuries. This region has been the place where invasions have been thwarted, turned back, resumed and finally broken through. Tamerlane himself twice tried unsuccessfully to break through this gap, and only did so when he brought up a second army, the first time he had to do so in all his conquests.

Not all movement came from the East. There were also invasions from Europe and Asia Minor: Greeks, Romans and Ottoman Turks and invasions from the North: Slavs and Caucasians. In the 19th century, this wave and counter-wave of invasion was resumed, this time between the Russian Empire and the Turkish Empire. In 1809, 1814, 1855, and again in 1877 there were wars between Russia and Turkey, and always the main brunt of the fighting was taken somewhere here. The frontier between the two countries has always run a little to the East or a little to the West of this point.

Because it is near a frontier, Kars has never been regarded as a safe place. It has been built and destroyed and rebuilt and destroyed again. The town itself—as all these towns round here—is filled with mounds of rubble. I am sure that all this has had a powerful effect on the psyche of the people of this part of the world. They have lived for centuries, if not for thousands of years, in a state of stress, never knowing when an attack was going to come from the East or from the West. And undoubtedly Gurdjieff himself was subject to this stress. One of the worst experiences of the city of Kars was in October 1877, when it was taken by the Russians and there was terrible destruction at that time. I have looked at the history both from the Russian and the Turkish point of view. According to the Turks, there was just a wild massacre on the part of the Russians which lasted for three days. The Russian history says that the Turks resisted in a very foolish way and that pockets of resistance were gradually wiped out, but probably the two stories refer to the same event.

Before 1877, Kars was a considerable town. It had over 20,000 inhabitants and round it was relatively rich country. It is nothing like so rich as it gets lower towards Tabriz, but still fertile. Kars was taken by assault by the Russians in 1877, and in the following year, when the Russians had to give up what they had taken away up here in the Balkans, they were confirmed in the retention of Batoum, Kars and Ardahan. At that time, about 80 per cent of the population was Turkish. After the Russian conquest there was a great exodus and about 80,000 Turks migrated westwards in the next two or three years, and the Russians themselves brought non-Turks from all over this part of the world. They brought Greeks who themselves wanted to leave Turkey. Armenians were brought in from the South Caspian region. Assyrians — Aisors as they are called there — were brought up from Iraq. Quite a considerable number of Yezidis were persuaded to migrate to the North and settle in this part of the world. Heterodox sects such as the Molokans and Dukhobors came from Russia and even Esthonian Lutherans. So that between 1877 and the early 1880's, there was an extraordinary mix-up in this part of the world. Tens of thousands of families were moved hither and thither against their will.

You must understand that all this moving about was part of the policy of these governments. No one knew what to do with the disaffected populations. The Russians did not know what to do with the large Muslim population that was hostile to the

Russian domination; the Turks did not know what to do with their large Christian population, which was equally hostile to them.

These were the conditions of Gurdjieff's boyhood. So far as I myself can make out from various sources, from what he himself and his family have told us, it does seem probable that he was born in 1872, in Alexandropol, and that his father moved to Kars soon after it was taken by the Russians, that is to say, somewhere about 1878, when he was six or so years old.

I do not know if you can picture the state of tension and distress that is caused by this kind of situation. I myself was in Greece in 1925, when there was the great exchange of populations. A million and a half Greeks were taken out of Asia Minor and dumped in Old Greece, and 400,000 Turks were taken from Macedonia and Thrace and dumped in Asia Minor. It was heartrending to see these unfortunate people being sent to a country with different geographical conditions, different ways of life from their own, with the jealousy of the population that was being asked to receive them, the difficulty of getting land for them to settle in. I expect that some of you will have seen the even more distressing migrations of Arabs in Jordan. You may have visited, as I have, the refugee camps there, or have seen in Damascus what happened to the unfortunate Kurds and Tartars and others who were moved down from the Black Sea coast. Only if you have seen it with your own eyes can you get a picture of the distress that there is in these forced movements of populations who do not understand why they are being moved or where they will end up.

Such things were happening in the Caucasus when Gurdjieff was a boy. He was only a child when the worst of it happened, and by the time he was six or seven years old, there is no doubt that things had begun to settle down. When his father moved to Kars, which had been reconstructed after the frightful destruction and carnage of October 1877, there was already some hope of peace and quiet.

There were other hardships to be borne, due to the severe climatic conditions. It is bitterly cold in the winter; it goes down to 30-40 degrees below freezing every winter and remains cold for several months, so that they have continual snow. There is a sudden thaw in the early spring, and about six weeks or two months of mud—which I can certify, having been there myself a couple months ago when you can hardly think of anything but the mud which surrounds you everywhere. Then comes the dry summer when all the mud turns to dust; and they have four or five months of intensely hot dry weather. These are not comfortable conditions of existence, especially for people who have got no satisfactory homes. At all times, as far as I can make out, the poorer population of Kars and of these other towns round about, have lived rather miserably in mud huts, sometimes under ground level, holes in the ground with roofs put over them and even a path going over the top of the roof. So that when you walk about, you sometimes do not know that you are walking on top of somebody's roof, until you see someone coming out below you.

These are the conditions as they are today. What it can have been like 80 or 90 years ago, I do not like to think. They must have been very bitter conditions. Gurdjieff in his own book, <u>Meetings with Remarkable Men</u>, does not to my mind really convey the sharpness of the conditions when he writes about his father and his first tutor. This is probably because he himself was so toughened by all the hardships that it did not seem to him anything special to write about. But I think you should have this picture of the severity of the conditions of existence, combined with the strain of war and the migration of populations, in order to picture to yourselves what a strange thing it is that out of all that a man could come who could make his mark on the world by intellectual power as well as psychic power that impressed so many hundreds of people, not themselves stupid, who came in contact with him.

You must look, however, at another side of this. That with this severity of physical and psychological conditions, also this part of the world is particularly richly endowed with traditional material. The population, when Gurdjieff was a boy, was, as I said, predominantly Muslim, and he learnt to talk Turkish from childhood. He talked Turkish, when I first knew him, better, I think, than he spoke Russian. Now the Turks, especially in the Eastern <u>vilayete</u>, are very devoted to the mystical side of Islam, to Sufism. There always have been many Dervish communities in this part of the world. There is no question that Gurdjieff was influenced by Islamic mysticism, but at the same time he was also in a region of strong Greek and Russian Christian spirituality. Thirdly, he was himself half Armenian for his mother was an Armenian. That part of the world was really more Armenian than anything. The Armenians begin to preponderate as soon as you cross over the valley where present-day Armenia now is. The Armenians have quite separate traditions from either the Western or the Greek and Russian Orthodox Christians. There is the very ancient Armenian tradition of which Nakhichevan is the sacred city. This Armenian tradition is blended with other, older, pre-Christian traditions. Not only that, there are the Assyrians, the descendants of the Chaldeans, the Aisors as they are called there. Various communities still exist which have preserved traces of the ancient Babylonian, Zoroastrian and Mithraic mysteries and mysticism. The Yezidis are a special branch, with which Gurdjieff came into contact, with their own form of the Babylonian dualistic belief in the conflict of two powers in the world—the powers of good and evil, which is the basis of the Zoroastrian tradition.

Not only these comparatively well-known, but also many obscure sects, existed then and still do exist there today. I wonder whether there is anywhere else in the world where one can point to such a variety of influences that a young man touched by the need for spirituality could come in contact as here in this part of the Caucasus. It is close to Iran, where a strong Sufi tradition remained then and certainly still remains to this day. It is close to Armenia, close also to the quite different mystical traditions of the Turkish Sufis. In a way, therefore, one can say that together with all the influences that would make life very hard, there was also, to anyone who could feel for it, a very rich fund of traditional beliefs and practices in that very environment in which Gurdjieff was born. He gives

some indications of all this in his own writings, in
the <u>Meetings with Remarkable Men</u>, which probably
most of you have read.

But between these two things, the very difficult conditions of life of a poor Greek-Armenian
boy living in the Greek quarter of Kars, barely able
to attend the newly built Russian town school, how
could any reconciling understanding arise? How
could he get a chance? One of the many strange
events in the story of Gurdjieff is that he began to
make contacts which could neither be ascribed to
his own personal background, his parentage, his
connection with the Greeks and Armenians, nor with
the sort of influences that would be surrounding him
in that Greek quarter - there were also, as I said,
people from the Assyrians and Molokans and so on,
but none of those—as I know from having seen in
other parts of this world—had anything to give that
could change Gurdjieff in the way he has been
changed. He came in contact, while still a boy,
with the Russian community, and by extraordinary
good fortune, with the Russian community surrounding the Russian Orthodox Church in Kars, the Church
that was established immediately after the conquest
in 1877 for the Russian Army of occupation. Most
of you will have read, and it would be a waste of
time for me to repeat, the story of his contact with
the Dean Borsh of the Military Cathedral and with
other priests of the Cathedral, and how they taught
him and of how he was able to develop some contact
with the Western culture of his time.

Now the interesting thing is that this, which
would have satisfied the ambitions of any young man
however determined he was to get on in the world,

according to Gurdjieff himself, did not correspond to his own ambitions. He wanted to become altogether Western. This is very understandable, and anyone of us who has been in the Asiatic countries, knows this strange craze that there is for becoming 'technical,' for turning young men into engineers or scientists, when they have talents of quite a different order. Gurdjieff was caught with the same craze, and wished to become an engineer or technician; but with all that, he came under these influences of the traditions, and they would not leave him alone.

We can picture Gurdjieff as a boy under various actions. First, were the severe conditions of his material environment and his human environment; second, the contact that he had with the Western culture through the Russian garrison of Kars, and third, the contact with the older traditions, which were, as he himself said, entirely in conflict with the Westernizing tendencies of the Russians with whom he was in contact. There is no doubt that through being subjected to such contrasting, apparently conflicting influences he was able to come to a realization that there was a great problem; and that is, to account for all the conflicting interpretations of the significance of human life. He was in front of the conflict between the Christian and the Islamic traditions. He was also subjected to the conflict of the kind of dualism which was inherent in the traditions of the Assyrians and the Yezidis, and the unitary traditions which were common to Christians and Muslims and Jews. He saw from early youth, a most significant conflict of beliefs between those of Monotheism and Ditheism; that is, between those who like the Jews, Christians and Muslims believed in one God, Supreme Ruler of the World, and those who like the Zoroastrian dualists believed in two equal and opposite powers. He also stood between East and West at the meeting point of Europe and Asia. He could see for himself how radically different were the two world views and he could also see that with all their divergent views and beliefs men were all the same. He saw spiritual men and materialists, those who looked for reality within and those who trusted only what they could see and hold. Who were right, and where were they all going? Such questions were real and burning questions, and they entered into Gurdjieff's life quite early in his youth.

Was there something in him that was able to see beyond what all those round him were seeing? He had written of his inner conviction that there must be some sense in it all; some sense which would take in the peculiar, even superstitious, beliefs of the old environment, without denying the very striking and extraordinary powers that were undoubtedly possessed by people of that part of the world; giving full weight to the other side, to the increasing domination of the world by the inventiveness and cleverness of man, looked upon at that time as the prerogative of Western Europe.

I think it is not possible to doubt that there was something very unusual in that boy. He himself was a divided character. It is evident from all the accounts he gives of his own boyhood and also from the traces that were left in the later years of his life, that he had in his character very much that we should regard as all too human. He was sensual, loving food, women and beauty, impatient, subject to fits of rage and passion. Moreover, he was ready, in order to satisfy his thirst for knowledge, to be quite unscrupulous in the way he would get it. On the other hand, he never at any time was really interested in possessions or in fame. Undoubtedly, he got himself into trouble more than once in his early years by trying to get knowledge that he was not entitled to, or before he was entitled to it.

With these defects of character, he also had a burning compassion for the sufferings of mankind, all the stronger because he soon became aware that these sufferings are due to our nature. So far as I can make out he was still under thirty when he came to the conclusion that the main cause of human suffering lies in defects that people do not take sufficiently into account. These are, especially, our own credulity and suggestibility, to both of which we are subject because of our vanity and egotism. He realized that we are in slavery to quite trivial and stupid forces that act on us, so that we cannot do the things that we wish to do and we find ourselves doing things that are against everything we hold to be right and to be necessary for man. Gurdjieff saw very deeply the significance of this strange and pitiable condition of mankind. He saw mankind not so much as evil, harmful, or dangerous, but as helpless. This led him to the feeling of a great need to find a way to help people to be delivered of this helplessness.

He also certainly had powers; what are commonly called "psychic powers." These must have been developed in him from unusual potentialities he inherited and was born with. He learned to develop his psychic powers by coming in contact with traditional teachings which, in that part of the world, possess a very extensive practical knowledge of the ways in which man can develop the latent psychic powers. The possession of such powers is a terrible temptation, and Gurdjieff saw that they were both necessary to him and also a danger. One of the touching features of his whole life was what he did to protect himself and others from his own unusual power to influence others. It was touching, because it meant a bitter struggle with his own nature. He must have been very tempted to use these powers for the attainment of his own ends and yet he was ready to sacrifice them quite ruthlessly rather than become their slave. In doing so, he made it impossible for himself to achieve certain tasks he set himself to do. That makes his life very hard to understand, because at times he appeared to be on the verge of achieving something very important and extraordinary, and then something would happen which would change the whole direction of his life. This is common enough with people to whom it happens through some weakness of their own; for example, when they suddenly fail to stand up to the moment of decision and lack in courage or persistence. It was not for such reasons that Gurdjieff failed; it was because of a certain peculiar fastidiousness which was hard to understand for people who only saw him from the outside. He had a certain fastidiousness about using ruthless methods. And that made it very difficult to understand him, because there were times when he really would act so ruthlessly as to terrify those around him. When he acted otherwise, it was not from fear or lack of decision;

but from the realization that to take another step would involve him in consequences which might give immediate benefits but would ultimately defeat the higher aim he had set himself.

All of that makes it hard to understand his life and I shall have to talk to you rather specially about the methods that he used in order to protect himself and other people from the powers that he himself had and could exercise. But tonight the main thing is to talk to you about his background, his early environment. So far, I have spoken only about the immediate boyhood environment, that is, the town of Kars, and the surrounding country.

By the time he was fourteen or fifteen, he was already beginning to travel. Not finding the answers to the questions in his own immediate society, not even among these cultivated Russians of the army of occupation in Kars, he began to look further afield. He certainly went both to Nakhichevan and Tabriz. Tabriz is very near to the frontier of Persia and it is very much a Turkish town. The people talk Turkish and are more of the Turkish race than Persian. In Tabriz and the mountains that surround it, there certainly has been a long persistent tradition—probably going back 3 or 4,000 years —and for people who have the good fortune to come in contact with it, there is still very much to be found in that part of the world. Gurdjieff has left clear indications that he found something important in North-West Persia.

Gurdjieff was also fascinated by his own maternal ancestry; that is, by the Armenians. The Armenians, during one period of the history of man, did carry a special torch, a certain culture, between

the 8th and 10th centuries, that very difficult period
for nearly the whole of the world. There were the
Bagratid Kings of Ani. Certainly the Armenians did
not reach this position of power without a long pre-
paratory period which goes back before the rise of
Islam and Gurdjieff was interested in the transition
from the Christian epoch in that part of the world to
the rise of Islam; because much was destroyed at
that time, and what was most important went under-
ground, and remained hidden in secret societies.
Gurdjieff, suspecting that they still existed, was
very intent upon tracing them. You will see refer-
ences to this in the Chapter, 'Pogossian,' in his
<u>Meetings with Remarkable Men</u>. That led him to a
journey down through Kurdistan, round Lake Van, to
Mosul on the Tigris.

I have visited Mosul once or twice. It is a
city where one gets the impression that there is
something ancient, something which has been going
on for a very long time; I believe it started long before the rise of Islam, even before Christianity.
Nearby are Nineveh and Nimrod, the cities of the
Assyrian power; but somehow it is not quite that.
The impression that I have myself is of something
that withdrew to that part of the world after the down-
fall of Babylon. Gurdjieff was in quest of this knowledge, which perhaps belonged to the Chaldeans.

I must jump now to another of his early influences; that is, the Greek Orthodox tradition. His
own father's family came from the Byzantine Greek
people. When the Ottoman Turks conquered Con-
stantinople in 1453, they left the whole structure of
the old Byzantine Empire; taking over and adapting
to their own needs what was needed to keep it all

going. They were at pains to ingratiate themselves with the Greek population, requiring the Greeks for the administration of this vast new empire that they were winning. So that there was a peculiar kind of tension; the Turks needing the Greeks and at the same time there was a resentment against the Greek culture. But it undoubtedly influenced them very greatly and also influenced the Sufis of that time. In a strange way, there was an interplay, and the place where a lot of extraordinary things certainly happened was Caesarea as it was then called, Kayseri now. Caesarea was one of the first cities to be converted to Christianity at the time of the missionary journeys and it is the place where the great Christian saints like St. Basil and St. John Chrysostom and St. Gregory lived and constructed the Liturgy of the Christian Church.

Before Christianity came, Cappadocia was a centre of the cult of Anahita, the Mother Goddess; who, strangely enough, made that very same journey from Persia right through Kars, having invaded and arrived in Asia Minor. With her—that is, with her priests, there came a great body of knowledge, and some of that knowledge, perhaps more than people can readily appreciate, has been brought into the construction of the Christian Liturgy. One could say much about the mystery of this Liturgy, which contains so much knowledge, so many hidden things; for this deeply impressed Gurdjieff and he wanted to understand what was being preserved for mankind behind the ritual of the Church. And for that, he made journeys to the Western world. At that time, there were still monasteries in Cappadocia. They remained from about the third century right on and on and on, through the Byzantine Empire, remaining after the Turkish conquest, right through until our day. For sixteen centuries there was a monastic tradition here in Cappadocia. Then it was abruptly stopped at the time when the whole of the population was expelled in 1925.

I am trying to convey to you what I personally believe, and that is, that there has been much more mutual enrichment of traditions than we usually suppose. This part of the world was a kind of crucible in which different traditions were blended, and out of them have come the forms that we now see as so separate—and even opposed to one another—of the Christian, the Islamic, Assyrian, Zoroastrian traditions and so on. All of this, you can well understand, would make a deep impression on a young man in search of the answer to the question: "Does it all make sense, is there a place for all these aspects of human experience, or must some be accepted and others rejected?" And also, the other question which was so sharp for Gurdjieff, "How is it that mankind, to whom so much has been given by the traditional teachings, and the revelations of the past 4 or 5,000 years, how is it that man has been able to make so little use of what he has received, and how is it that he remains under the domination of forces which are quite alien to the real meaning of his own life?"

I think that these Westward searches of Gurdjieff's brought him still further West; first to Istanbul, then to the Holy Land, to Egypt, and even to Abyssinia, where he found again another place where there are strange contacts with lost traditions. Whether he went any further South into Ethiopia, I do not know, but I do know that Ethiopia was very important to him because to the very end of his life he spoke of his great love for Ethiopia. Once he said that he thought of going to spend the rest of his days there. He said that the two places where he felt he had ties were one, Central Asia, that is, Bokhara, and the other Ethiopia. If that is so and if he was not pulling our legs—which of course he often did—it would mean that his visits to Ethiopia formed quite an important part of his total searches. Then of course there were his searches in Central Asia. About those, because they are closely connected with his subsequent teaching, I have to speak about next week. There is little doubt that it was in Central Asia that he came across what was most distinctive and important in what he subsequently called his 'Ideas,' and other people called his 'System.' It is only by making a fairly thorough search into the Central Asian traditions, that we can hope to answer the question: did all that he taught come from these parts of the world, or was there something that was distinctively his own? *

Editor's note: At this point, Mr. Bennett showed pictures of Kars, Ani, etc.

QUESTIONS

Q. May I ask if the Mother Goddess, who is said to be Anahita and was worshipped in that area, is the same as Lilith who was both good and evil?

J.G.B. No, I do not think so. It is the same as Cybele who was brought to Rome. Lilith belonged to a more ancient time than this. The important thing, in my opinion, is that there was a continuous tradition in that part of Cappadocia.

• • •

Q. Was Gurdjieff remembered in his own country and territory?

J.G.B. No, there are no Christians left in Kars, as far as I know, not one. When I spoke about him, nobody had heard of his name, and when people heard that I had made this long and arduous journey to this derelict country town out of respect for the memory of Gurdjieff, they thought that I was quite crazy. I should say that I did search for the place referred to in his writings where his first tutor Dean Borsh was buried, but everything was so destroyed and smashed up in 1918 and again in 1920, that nothing can really be traced any more.

I think that Gurdjieff is known a little further East than this, that memories of him remain round about Tabriz. The people who might know about Gurdjieff would be some of the Dervish sects of that part of the world, but I did not have time to get in touch with them. This cannot be done in a hurry. Further West, when I was in Istanbul, I did both meet and talk with two or three of the Dervish Brotherhood. They retained very long memories of things that have happened. But I was not really in search of this.

• • •

Q. How does it come that <u>Meetings with Remarkable Men</u> was published so long after his death?

J.G.B. He died on October 29th, 1949, not fourteen years ago yet. He was not very clear about expressing his wishes about the publication of his second series, that is <u>Meetings with Remarkable Men</u>, but he was very clear that he wanted the first book, <u>Beelzebub</u>, to be published. He said the <u>Meetings with Remarkable Men</u> was to be read aloud, but only to those who had assimilated <u>Beelzebub</u>. I shall say more about it next week; but it is a much more difficult book than most people realize. Those who have not seen what he is after in this book, and who read it just as a kind of autobiographical account, or as amusing escapades, can have no idea at all of the purpose of the book. Or, if they expect to find in the book some part of his practical teaching, they also are mistaken, because it has no claim to contain that. But what it contains is really very important, and hardly anyone has understood this. It is probable that the time was not ready, had not come yet for this. The great thing is that it is now available to all.

• • •

Q. You have given us tantalizing things about the contents of the <u>Meetings with Remarkable Men</u>. Can you not say more?

J.G.B. Next Monday I will show you just how I
followed up one particular clue and you will see in
that how unlikely it is that anyone who has not got
considerable knowledge both of Gurdjieff's own ways
of doing things and also of this part of the world,
would have seen what the clue was. If you see that
one there, you will see what is involved in being
able to decipher the rest of it, because in reality
the <u>Meetings with Remarkable Men</u> is written in a
kind of cipher, and one has to know how to decipher
it. One may think, why should one bother? That
all depends whether you wish to get to the bottom
of it or not.

. . .

Q. Do you understand the languages spoken in that
part of the world?

J.G.B. Yes, that is why I go there. I get stuck if
I go further East. Languages make all the difference. All the way across Asia, you can talk Turkish; right past the Caspian Sea, across the Amu
Daria, right into Chinese Turkestan they can talk
some dialect of Turkish. When I was a young man,
if you knew Turkish, you could find people who
could understand you all the way from the Adriatic
right through to the wall of China. When I was living in that part of the world in 1919-20, I had the
job of interviewing the Muslim pilgrims who came
through from Central Asia and I was very astonished
to find that I could talk to people like Sarts and
Uzbegs. I was able to talk with them, because
these different Turkish dialects are more like one
another certainly than, say, English, Dutch and

German. It is worth mentioning that Gurdjieff, who certainly could talk Turkish quite easily, for some reason or other pretended that the language spoken here is Persian. If any of you have read the Introduction to <u>Meetings with Remarkable Men</u>, where he speaks about philological questions, and says how strange it is that in English they use one word to express <u>say</u> or something like this, whereas in Persian they use two quite different words, and he talks of the words <u>diyaram</u> and <u>soilyaram</u>. That is simply a very strange way of writing two perfectly good Turkish words as spoken here in Kars, the Turkish of his boyhood. But in the book he calls it Persian. If you understand why Gurdjieff should pretend that what is perfectly good Turkish is Persian you will understand the way he disguises things. I do not believe myself that he knew so many languages. When I first heard of him in 1919, he was spoken of as a man who had travelled all over the East and knew many languages, but I do not think so. I say this because Turkish will take you almost anywhere. At the end of the 19th century you could travel all over Central Asia with Turkish. He would not learn anything else until he got over towards Tibet, and then you had to begin to learn something new, and he certainly set himself quite industriously to learn Tibetan. But I should imagine that he probably knew only Turkish and had acquired some Turkish dialects and also Tibetan. But that is about all. But that will take you a long way in these parts.

THE SOURCES OF GURDJIEFF'S IDEAS

Our next task is the attempt to reconstruct searches that Gurdjieff made between the middle 1880's and about 1910. After 1910, he had found what he was looking for, and was prepared to transmit it to others.

The first thing to remember about Gurdjieff is that he was born of a Greek father and an Armenian mother. Therefore he certainly had contact with the Greek and the Armenian Churches, as well as with the Russian Church—all of which were represented in his home town of Alexandropol and the town where he lived in his early childhood, that is, the town of Kars.

There are one or two things I have to say about the influence of such a childhood teaching. To my mind one of the principal differences, psychologically, between the Eastern and the Western Churches, is that the Eastern Church insists principally on the notion of death and resurrection, of dying with Christ and rising again with Christ. This Easter message is the central theme of the Eastern Church, both in its ritual and also—if one may say so—in its psychology. This has had a visible effect upon people of the Eastern Churches, and accounts for their preoccupation with death and its significance. In the West, we do not have this to the same degree; our Christian belief and our Christian practices are more concerned with sin and redemption, with union with Christ, than with dying and rising again. Substantially, at the bottom, the belief is no doubt the same throughout——I am only speaking now of a particular emphasis, which one feels very much when one is in contact with people of the Eastern Christianity.

There is, I think, also perhaps, in the Eastern Churches a particularly profound sense of the mystery of religion, and of the reality of an unseen element in all religious practice and experience. This does not mean again, of course, that the Western Churches are less mystical than the Eastern Churches, but that the mysticism of the Eastern Churches is more mystery-mysticism than illumination-mysticism, which belongs more to the Western. I think it is fair to say that this early religious background left its mark on Gurdjieff, as it must do on all who are brought up in similar conditions. That is all that I am able to say about this. He himself has said that he continued to be influenced, not only through his boyhood, but later, by his contact with monks of the Orthodox Church——Russian and Greek monks also. He claimed that one of his earliest teachers and friends had entered into a particularly mysterious brotherhood that he called the Brotherhood of the Essenes, of whom he said that their chief monastery still existed not far from the Dead Sea.

It is probable that Gurdjieff retained his contact with the Greek and Russian Orthodox tradition throughout the whole of his life, and certainly when I saw him at the end of his life, the sense that he was a member of the Russian Orthodox Church was quite strong with us. But he was also half Armenian and his mother-religion was the Armenian. This is substantially different from the Greek and Russian, from the Eastern Churches that we commonly regard as 'Orthodox.' The Armenian Church, which has a very ancient Christian tradition, contains elements that perhaps the other Christian Churches have since lost—elements that go back to the early centuries, and belong to that powerful and extraordinary Christian tradition that penetrated from Syria into Mesopotamia, into the old Persia, and right up the valleys of the Euphrates and the Tigris into Central Asia. This very widespread Christian tradition, which was neither Orthodox nor Roman, was overrun by Islam in the 8th century, and has only left traces which we know as the Nestorian and Assyrian Christians. But we must not forget that in the early centuries, this branch of the Christian tradition was as important as either the Greek or the Roman Churches. This was brought home to me when in 1953 I visited the valleys of the Euphrates and Tigris, and particularly met an extremely learned man—perhaps the greatest scholar in this particular field—in Mosul. I was able to enter into that tradition to some extent by visiting some of the oldest monasteries belonging to the Armenian and Assyrian and Nestorian Christianity—of which of course only the ruins remain at this time—and also by meeting the Nestorians, Assyrian and Armenian Christians.

I am saying all this because I think that we tend very often to forget that up to the 7th century, the Christianity of the Middle East was a very important part of the whole Christian life, and only failed to reintegrate with the West, because of the arising of Islam and the interpenetration which then took place between the Islamic, the Persian and the Christian traditions in that part of the world. We commonly use the word 'Eastern' for the Greek and Russian Chruches, and tend to forget the importance of the Armenian, Assyrian, Nestorian and other churches of those early days. But certainly Gurdjieff did not forget this, and he was powerfully influenced by the realization that something had been preserved in the Armenian Church and also among the Assyrian and Nestorians, which was connected with the process of spiritual transformation of man, which they, in their turn, had probably inherited from the earlier traditions of the Chaldeans, with which, to a great extent, we have lost contact.

Those of you who have read Gurdjieff's autobiographical writings, the <u>Meetings with Remarkable Men</u>, recently published in this country, will have noticed how he was convinced that there was a knowledge that belonged to this Assyrian—as he called it, Aisor—tradition, that was important from the practical point of view. It possessed certain spiritual methods and exercises, and insights into the hidden nature of man, that he could not find in his contact with the now predominant Eastern and Western Christian Churches.

One effect of this was to direct Gurdjieff's attention back towards the past, where he could hope to find perhaps the traces to what was now largely lost. There are others who have come to that conclusion, that the inner, or spiritual, tradition, has largely been lost by the Western Churches —such as, for example, René Guénon—but, I am not here to speak about that. I am simply speaking now about Gurdjieff's own situation when he was still a boy between 15 and 18 years old, and experienced the very intense need both to understand the meaning of life and also to find how one could lift oneself out of this situation in which he saw all the people of his environment — Greeks, Armenians, Russians, Tartars, Turks and others.

Now another side of his Armenian parentage, of the contacts that he had through his mother, is the importance among the Armenians of secret societies. Armenians also have an unrivalled talent for keeping out of notice, so that it is only when some unexpected events occur, that cannot be explained by the visible forces, that one begins to suspect that perhaps some pawn has been moved on the board by the hand of an Armenian secret society. I am speaking as one who has lived much in the Near and Middle East — I am not saying that this occurs so much in Western Europe. The point as far as Gurdjieff is concerned, is that through the Armenian secret societies he had an unrivalled opportunity, for a young man, of travelling. This is connected with what I was saying last week, about this extraordinary phenomenon of Gurdjieff's coming out of Kars from the terrible and miserable environment of these invasion-ridden areas of the Caucasus. One contributing factor to his emancipation from this was no doubt the possibility of moving about and opening up contacts quite a considerable distance from his own home, through the Armenian secret societies, sometimes actually as their messenger or representative. Then he describes himself in one of the chapters of his book, the chapter called 'Pogossian,' his Armenian friend with whom he went first to Etchmiasin, the holy city of the Armenians, and afterwards down to Kurdistan and, according to his own story, ended by going Westward into the Holy Land instead of Eastward into Mosul, as he originally planned. But there is no doubt, of course, that that Eastward journey into Mosul was made later. I have myself heard him speak about Mosul as one of the most interesting and important places in the world still. And I am sure that all of you who have been to that part of the Tigris valley have felt the mystery of Mosul and the surrounding country. It is not just a contact with a dead past, but something which has never ceased and is still somehow there, though perhaps now disappearing. Something still remained in Gurdjieff's time and had been there for not less than 3,000 and perhaps as much as 4,000 years in an unbroken tradition. I know that other people who have been into Mosul and the surrounding country have had the same impression that there is something strange there, if only one could find it. Gurdjieff was not one to have that feeling and not set about in a very determined way to find what he smelt was somewhere hidden. From Mosul Northward into Kurdistan, to Urmia and the crossing into Persia there has been, and probably still is, much to be found by people who have the necessary qualities. But I should warn you that these qualities are not given to everyone.

This part of the story is really concerned with the awakening of Gurdjieff to the conviction that a real tradition had existed in the Middle East; possessing knowledge of man, of the world, and also

of certain methods and techniques which have remained intact through the great changes due to the
invasions that have come from Central Asia and also
through the great changes of religion.   First, the
replacement of the Zoroastrian——the major tradition
——by the Christian, and then again the Christian
largely overrun by the Muslim. And yet, through it
all, something remained, what is more, as the waves
of invasion have come and gone——Genghis Khan and
Tamerlane and Atabeg and the rest of them. The
waves returning to Central Asia have carried back
with them always something, and therefore there is
little doubt——and nobody can question this——that in
Central Asia, in the parts called Turkestan, there
has been and is a tradition which no doubt survived
even with the present regime of the Soviet Republic
there.

Now, we come to certain more specific indications about the way in which Gurdjieff traced
this back and no doubt found something. He travelled
with a group of people whom he called 'The Seekers
of the Truth' and some of whom he characterizes
quite definitely and has spoken of since as people
who were still living even ten or fifteen years ago.
Probably the stories told in Meetings with Remarkable
Men are genuine enough, though I know, from a certain amount that I have been able to verify, they are
all mixed up. In other words, he takes one particular story and puts a bit of it here and another bit
there. Certain parts of it also appear in the first
book; that is, in Beelzebub, or the first part of All
and Everything, which has now been published for
thirteen years. There are there——as everyone can

see for themselves certain autobiographical sections which are a clue to his own wanderings and his own findings.

One of the things which it is possible to do if you have that luck, or that quality or whatever it is when you are travelling through these parts of the world, is to run unexpectedly into very interesting people. This has happened to me a number of times. I never can understand why it is that something has led me to such a village and I have gone into such a valley and unexpectedly met a person, or I have heard at one place that I ought to go and see so and so and have found a man selling secondhand clothes in a little village, and it turns out that he is an initiated Dervish and so on. These things happen to some people, and they do not happen to other people. I do not know why. I should think they probably happened to me because I had a good deal of preparation and training through my contact with Gurdjieff over so many years. I know that it does happen, and certainly must have happened to Gurdjieff, that in the course of his travels, without any plan, without knowing what he was going to find, he or one of his companions, would hear of something or someone and follow up the clue. This would lead them into the presence of someone who had knowledge, or who had understanding, or perhaps certain powers. Such people very often are not visibly connected with any organization or brotherhood. I have been misled in this way, because I have met people who said that they were not connected with anything at all; just living a solitary and happy life as a recluse in a valley; experiencing the reality of their own inner life or the Presence of God, and not looking for anything more. And then several years later, I would discover that that person, who seemed to be a solitary recluse, was really quite an important member of some brotherhood or other.

Gurdjieff, with his flair for this kind of search, would not only recognize the significance of each such contact; but would also be able to piece the fragments together to build up a coherent picture.

I am now going to tell you about two discoveries which I think will illustrate how Gurdjieff left clues behind so that anyone who diligently and intelligently studies his writings can find some indications; and perhaps—if they feel the need to do so—trace them back to the source. The first is the existence in a region that stretches from East to North-East to North-West Persia across into Kurdistan, of a sect or brotherhood called 'The People of the Truth,' the Ahl-i-Haqq. This sect has been known for a long time. It is referred to in Hastings' Encyclopaedia of Religion and Ethics in several places; but always in passing and rather disparagingly as a heterodox Shiite sect of Persia. It is generally supposed that they are somehow connected with the Ali Ilahis, which is a very extreme Shiite sect who deify Ali, the son-in-law of Muhammad. One would not expect anything of great interest from that, but if you take the fact that they are called 'The People of the Truth' together with Gurdjieff's reference to his own groups as the 'Seekers of the Truth,' you might perhaps guess that these people, this particular sect, were among those whom Gurdjieff sought and found. It so happens that he does not make any direct reference to a Persian brotherhood in any of his writings that you are likely to have seen, unless you happen to have come across a very rare book published in 1934, called The Herald of Coming Good. This is his first book and the only one published during his lifetime. In it he writes openly of his contact with a brotherhood in Persia, and says that he sent a number of his pupils to their monastery.

Now, I think it is very probable that this brotherhood is the same as the Ahl-i-Haqq with which I accidentally came in contact about seven or eight years ago when I was travelling in North-West Persia and with which I have had further contact since. The important thing about this particular brotherhood is that they certainly are in possession of technical knowledge of a very special kind; that is to say, it is not just a religious, more or less heretical sect of Islam, but it actually does preserve some very ancient traditions. The sect was founded in 1316 A.D. by Sultan Sahaq, but this was more a fresh start or reform than a true beginning. This is evident from the fact that they preserved, through the coming of Islam, not only Nestorian Christian traditions but also much earlier Chaldean or Zoroastrian traditions that had belonged to the time of the greatness of Babylon, which is now 4,000 years before the present. This Gurdjieff does refer to in his book The Herald of Coming Good. I had a very amusing example of the difficulty of knowing where one stands with Gurdjieff over this. One day, in July 1949, when I was with him in Paris, he said that he was going to make some Persian pilaff with real Persian rice which had been flown over to him from Persia. Now we were quite used to Gurdjieff informing us that he was going to bring in some exotic fruit that had been flown to him from the Solomon Islands, when people present in the room had been with him to the Halles that morning and had bought them with him in the French fruit market. When he said that the brinza cheese was specially flown to him from the Caucasus we knew that he always bought it from a particular Jewish shop in Paris. So we were naturally inclined to suppose that it was most unlikely that rice would have been flown to him from Persia. However, I went into his kitchen, and there I saw twenty or thirty little sacks all with labels and Persian stamps on them, and saw that he had, in fact, received by airmail a consignment of Persian rice. What is more, he had received it from the town of Kirmanshah, which happens to be just the very place which is near the centre of this particular brotherhood Ahl-i-Haqq. This may mean anything or nothing, and I must warn you that for anyone who reads Gurdjieff and tries to reconstruct anything about Gurdjieff's adventures, almost anything he writes may mean anything or nothing.

But there are certain much more serious reasons for supposing that there was in North-West Persia at that time—perhaps still is today—a knowledge that contributed towards Gurdjieff's own development. This knowledge is chiefly concerned with the transformation of energies. I am assuming that you would not have come here to hear these lectures unless you were already students of Gurdjieff's ideas and have read his books and the books about him, so I am not going to trouble to explain the teachings and ideas of Gurdjieff, but try to show you how it is possible in some way to follow his method of giving hints so that one can find one's way back to his sources. If so, you must know that a very central feature, or theme, of Gurdjieff's teaching and methods is that man is destined, or required, during his life on earth, to transform energies. One way of looking to see the reason of man's existence on the earth, is that he is able to produce, by his way of living, certain substances required for very high purposes. Man, through his fulfilling this task, receives in return an imperishable something for himself. In other words, that there is the task for man of transforming energies by the way he lives his life. That transformation, in some way or another, results in a division into three parts: one part of the energy has to be used up in performing the work that is needed; a second part of the energy goes to a particular purpose, where it is required; but the third part is his own reward, and enters into his own being and serves for the formation of his own vessel, or his own soul.

Now this goes back into the past—I think that this doctrine was held by the Chaldeans up to the time of the destruction of Babylon, and probably after that remained with the Eastern Christians about which I was talking to you—this required that there should be some knowledge of the sort of work, of the way of living, that makes it possible for man to fulfill this task. It is rather interesting, I think, to note that this is most specifically and clearly understood among the Christians of the old Tradition of the Near East. It is also understood by the Orthodox Christians but less understood by the Western Christians. For example, the Eastern Fathers, and particularly I think, the Russians, understood very clearly that there is something that is required of man of this kind, and they associated it with the idea of, that is, in order to participate in the Resurrection, a man has to acquire a Resurrection Body. Of course St. Paul teaches this in his epistles – but this notion of the need to acquire for oneself a Resurrection Body in order to participate in the Resurrection, was, I think, most strongly and clearly perceived, in the Eastern Christian world. And of course, this agrees with the interpretation given by the Eastern Christians of the Parable of the Wedding Garment; that there are two elements in salvation: there is the gratuitous acceptance of man through his Redemption whereby he is enabled to participate in the Feast, but there is also the requirement that is placed upon man himself, that he should come to the Feast with the Wedding Garment, which is interpreted as meaning the Resurrection Body. And that Resurrection Body is associated with the idea of the transformation of the fine spiritual substances that are exempt from the destructive forces of this earthly existence, and therefore able to participate in Resurrection.

This, I am sure, is somehow connected with the knowledge that is possessed by the Ahl-i-Haqq of whom I have spoken. It seems that they know the ways by which these energy transformations are brought about; that is, by which man is able, by his own way of living—which of course can take the outward forms of prayer and meditation but in reality consist in bringing about within himself a certain interaction of substances—whereby he fulfils his own particular task. All of you who have read Gurdjieff's writings will recognize that this is a central theme. He refers to it as the Reciprocal Maintenance of Everything that Exists. According to this

principle everything that exists is required to con-
tribute towards the existence of everything else.
There is a close and intimate interlocking of all
lives and all forms of life, by which each one is
required to do something for every other. What has
to be done in this way depends upon the transformation of energy. My own guess is that this is something Gurdjieff learnt through contacts made in those
parts of the Middle East that for millennia have been
called Iran. Hence also his deep interest in Babylon. Nobody can read what Gurdjieff writes about
Babylon without seeing how deeply it impressed him.
He was very fortunate because he was able to visit
Babylon at the time the German excavations were
in progress and when a great deal more of the old
city was accessible than it is now. Fortunately for
me, those excavations were made in the old style,
that is, instead of shutting everything up after dig-
ging it out, they left it open, and so I was able to
wander about in Babylon and get impressions from it.

I do not know if those of you who know Babylon have had so strongly as I had, the conviction
that a certain substance does remain now in Babylon by which one can enter directly into contact with
the life of the people about 2,500 to 3,000 years
ago. Each time I have been to Babylon, I have had
this unmistakably. I have been with others, and I
have noticed that some people notice nothing at all
when they go to Babylon; they see only a rather dull
lot of ruins. Other people are overwhelmed by the
sense of the unbroken life that is still going on in
this place that has been deserted for a thousand odd
years. Why is that? I think it is because there has
been for a very long time in this part of the world,

understanding of these substances and energies, and that the Babylonians did understand this. This work was intensively carried on in certain areas of Babylon, and it left behind almost imperishable traces of that particular work. This makes it possible for people, even today, to re-enter into contact with what was going on 2,500 or 3,000 years ago. In a sense it is still going on today.

You know that in <u>All and Everything</u> Gurdjieff describes several times the visits of Beelzebub in Babylon. They are among the most vivid writings in the book, and there are hardly any other places in the world that he describes with such a sense of being present in them. I did not see the significance of this until I visited Babylon myself and had the same sense of being able to be present in the living city. I thought how easy it must have been for Gurdjieff to re-enter the life of Babylon and meet the Babylonian people, and know the way they spoke and the sort of lives they lived and what were the motives that governed them and so on. And of course, all this would establish in him very strongly the sense of the importance of understanding how these transformations were to be brought about; how man really could learn to gain control over these psychic and spiritual energies or finer substances, both for his own benefit, for the feeding of his own individuality and also for the accomplishment of tasks that had to be done in the world. And also for other purposes too, such as the helping of individual people.

Gurdjieff undoubtedly had great natural gifts from childhood: but he probably was able as a very young man to develop, through his contact with these sources of knowledge, his powers to a considerable degree and then began to go further afield, having the sure and right instinct that a deeper and more important knowledge existed in Central Asia.

In order to be able to travel, in order to be able to make the necessary contacts, he tells us that he set himself up as a professional healer sometimes even as a professional wonder-worker, or miracle-man, and sometimes just as a hypnotist. He describes how very much he was able to do in Central Asia where at that time there was a very great addiction in the Russian areas to alcoholism, and in the Central and Eastern parts to opium smoking. Opium makes a special impression. I have been through miles and miles of poppy field in that part of the world, and was made to feel how strange and important is the place of the poppy plant for understanding human life. What it has done for man —opening up new possibilities for him, and also the terrible results of misusing the particular fine substance which is produced by the poppy plant. Anyhow, whatever it is, there is no doubt that Gurdjieff at the end of the last century, as a very young man, had found, through his knowledge of these transformations of substances, that he was able to help people with these two curses; the Russian curse of alcoholism and the Asiatic curse of addiction to opium. I myself remember, when I first met him in Istanbul in 1920, how he had in hand a most difficult and extraordinary case, when he cured a drunkard who was considered to be totally incurable.

This phase of Gurdjieff's life between 1895 and 1900 must certainly have been very extraordinary. Sometimes he was just going about in this part of the world with his fluent knowledge of Turkish, no doubt acquiring all the time facility with the various dialects of the Sart, the Uzbek, the Uigur and other races of Turkestan, and becoming known as a man who could help with what we now call psychosomatic ailments of man. In this he was motivated partly by the very real desire to help and do good to people, but more strongly by the necessity for understanding the hidden parts of the human psyche, which ordinarily are hidden behind the mask of our personality, and out of the reach of our ordinary consciousness. It is well known that this mask is either weakened or sometimes even destroyed in conditions of alcoholism and severe drug-addiction when something totally different very often appears. It certainly can be a means for more rapidly understanding the human psyche. Obviously, if Gurdjieff had the power to help people under those conditions, he would also become like a confidant or confessor to them. Many people would come to him in need, and in that way, during those years, he was undoubtedly engaged in what one might call the study of practical psychology. He himself says that before he started on these journeys and before he made his headquarters in Turkestan, he had studied everything that he could of Western psychology and had come to the conclusions that it had very little to offer in the way of explanations. I must remind you that this refers to Western psychology as it was in the 1890's.

He tells us that at some time or other, about the turn of the century, he was in Tibet. I think this is probably true, as I am sure that he knew more than a smattering of Tibetan. Colloquial Tibetan is not difficult to learn. It is mainly a matter of vo-

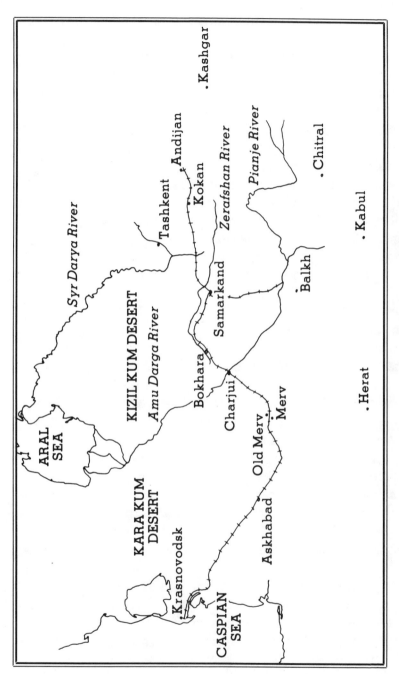

GURJIEFF'S CENTRAL ASIAN JOURNEYS

cabulary because the colloquial grammar of Tibetan is easy. If you do not want to learn to write it—which is a nightmare—to talk Tibetan is simple. I am sure it was well within Gurdjieff's compass to become familiar enough. Of course, Tibetan is not spoken only in Tibet. It is spoken on the other side of the mountains in Turkestan. It is also spoken southward in Nepal, as I have seen for myself. So it is a fairly widely-spoken language in one or other of its dialects, and would come in extremely useful for anyone wishing to travel in that part of the world.

Gurdjieff's visits to Tibet between 1899 and 1902 are connected with one of his severe accidents. He describes in one of the writings of the Third Series how he was wounded by a stray bullet during the Tibetan expedition. This made it necessary for him to spend a long time in recovering his strength. He was again severely wounded in 1904, at the time of the abortive Russian Revolution in the Caucasus —always, as he says, by stray bullets. Each time, apparently, he went to Central Asia where he had friends who understood about the curing of people through the use of these energies and substances. According to his own account, his injuries were such that without this sort of help, he would have died before he was thirty.

Now comes a very interesting question. I have spoken until now of the techniques connected with energies, with the transformation of substances and the deep study of human psychology by the use of Gurdjieff's knowledge of hypnotism and his power to deal with the troubles of mankind. But he also had a very extraordinary and profound knowledge of laws of the structure of the world and the human psyche. One must ask oneself; Where could he have found this knowledge?

When we were interested in these subjects in the middle 1920's, a group of us tried to trace, if possible, the sources of Gurdjieff's notions about Cosmic Laws. For example, his idea of what is called 'The Table of Hydrogens,' that is, the range of substances, from the finest, or Divine Substance, down to the coarsest substance that he called 'Matter without the Holy Ghost.' No doubt you are familiar with this from Ouspensky and Nicoll. Now obviously, this can be directly connected with Plato, and with the sesquialteral calculations given in Plato's <u>Timaeus</u> to arrive at the substances by which the Demiurge made the different worlds. These Platonic notions, after passing through neo-Platonism, entered into various semi-occult traditions such as the Rosicrucians of Europe and Free-Masonry, and more generally with what is commonly called occult tradition. The obvious similarity of these notions and the use made of them by the Rosicrucian authors of the 16th century, such as Dr. Robert Fludd, would make one at first think that Gurdjieff's cosmology is nothing more than an ingenious use of the Rosicrucian material of the 16th century, particularly that of the very important and powerful Rosicrucian School that existed in Holland at that time, of which Dr. Fludd was probably an associate member.

We read as much as we could of this rather laborious material—laborious because it is nearly all written in Latin, but fortunately with ample diagrams. And of course there is the well known <u>Aurora</u> of Jacob Bohme, with the remarkable diagrams constructed by William Law. I expect that this is the material on which Gurdjieff drew. But we came to a stop at a certain point when we realized that there was no indication of an understanding of what Gurdjieff called the Enneagram, or the nine-lined symbol which he used for the expression of this material. And, most important of all—although you do find in these Rosicrucian writers, particularly, let us say, in Dr. Fludd—the musical scale used, even three octaves in the way Gurdjieff uses them, there is no indication anywhere that the significance of what Gurdjieff calls the intervals, is understood in the way that Gurdjieff understood it. The important point for him is that it is necessary that there should be shocks, or independent interventions, in order to complete any process. This is really of very great importance, and I know from my own studies over many years that there is no doubt that by this a most important light is thrown upon our own personal experience, on the success and failure of all sorts of human enterprises, upon an understanding of the nature of living organisms and of the universe as a whole. All of this is only feebly understood if one does not take intervals and shocks into account.

It happened that just today—quite by accident not intending to read anything of this kind—I read the concluding passages of Kepler's treatise on the movements of the planets.* His work, as you

---

*The book is Johannes Kepler's Cosmographic Treatise containing the Secret of the Universe based on numbers and the sizes of the celestial spheres—all explained in terms of the five regular geometric figures. Tubingen 1596. This amazing document is translated by I. de Lubicz in The Egyptian Miracle, pp. 151-163.

know, was largely based upon the feeling that these Rosicrucian constructions must have cosmological significance. I had never previously read the final hymn with which Kepler ends his book. I had not realized how extraordinary was Kepler's attitude towards his own work. Kepler was looking for something. He, and also, of course, our own Isaac Newton, all of these men who founded the mechanical sciences and modern mathematics and astronomy, all of them were inspired by the belief that there was a Law of Harmony. Newton's library contained almost everything that was available at that time on this field——yet there was no sign that he knew this particular secret of the discontinuity of transitions and the need for shocks.

Now that does raise a really interesting question. Where did Gurdjieff find this if it was not known at the time when European thought was most closely concerned with this particular problem, that is, in the 16th and 17th centuries? Why is it that there is no sign among the neo-Platonists and no sign in pseudo-Dionysius, or in the Rosicrucian or Masonic traditions, of an understanding of the necessity of an interlocking play of processes in the way that Gurdjieff represents it in his symbol of the Enneagram?

Gurdjieff himself gives a clue to the solution because both in his book, <u>Beelzebub</u> and also in the writings of the second series, particularly in the chapter called 'Prince Yuri Lubovedsky,' he describes how he found his way to a particular brotherhood which he said was in Upper Bokhara, where this particular knowledge was available. You may not see that he refers to this particular knowledge——but if you will read again the section of the chapter which deals with the training of the priestesses who performed the sacred dances, and the apparatus that they used for their training, you will see that this is an unmistakable reference to this symbol of the Enneagram. Just in case any of you do not know this symbol, I will draw it on the board. It is made by taking a circle and dividing it into nine equal parts. The nine points are joined to give a triangle and a six-sided figure.

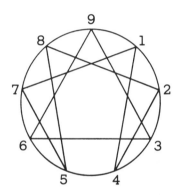

This is Gurdjieff's symbol of the Enneagram, which as you see, combines the triad and the hexad. The secret of the latter lies in the order of the points: 1, 4, 2, 8, 5, 7. The symbol shows how it is necessary that processes should lock together, each one supporting the other in order that anything stable should be achieved. This gives, for example, the stability of a living organism such as the body of man.

I think you will agree that if we could only establish where Gurdjieff found the Enneagram, we would understand where he found what is most important about the content of his teaching. It would tell us where he found that which is missing in the Western Tradition.

Now I have to tell you a very interesting sort of detective-story. Gurdjieff, in the story of 'Soloviev,' which is inserted in the middle of the Lubovedsky chapter, speaks of his being put on the way of finding what he himself was looking for and also of finding his own friend, Prince Yuri, through contact with a Bokharian Dervish, who is called Bogga-Eddin. Now Bogga-Eddin clearly was a Muslim, but there is no Muslim name Bogga-Eddin. There is no problem here, because Russians almost invariably transliterate H by G—they say 'gospital' when we say 'hospital,' for example—and they would almost certainly transliterate Bahauddin as Bogga-Eddin. Therefore, when Gurdjieff speaks of a Bokharian Dervish Bogga-Eddin, undoubtedly he is referring to someone called Bahauddin. Now, there is one extremely famous Bahauddin Naqshbandi of Bokhara, whose tomb there is famous in all Asia, and who is so venerated from the 14th century onward that it is said by Paul Vambery that three visits to the tomb of Mohammed Bahauddin Naqshbandi would be equivalent to a pilgrimage to Mecca.

So I think it is pretty certain that when Gurdjieff writes about the Bokharian Dervish Bogga-Eddin, he is putting us on to the Naqshbandi Order of Dervishes. Now, I must tell you that the Naqshbandi Order of Dervishes has fascinated me for many years. I have come across them all over the world.

Many of you have probably not even heard of the Naqshbandi before you heard me speak about them. Many people have heard of the Mevlevi, or Whirling Dervishes, the Rufai, or Howling Dervishes, or the Kadiri Dervishes, descended from Abdul Kadir Jelani; but I would be surprised—unless you have travelled in those parts—that you have heard much about the Naqshbandi. And yet, the Naqshbandi Order is at this present time by far the most widely distributed of all the Dervish Orders. Naqshbandi Dervishes can be found all the way from Morocco right through to Indonesia. This latter I happened to learn through Mohammed Subuh, who himself went as a boy to study with the most famous Naqshbandi Dervish Sheikh in Java called Abdurrahman. I believe that I am right in saying that there are Naqshbandi Dervishes even in the Solomon Islands. They certainly are in Pakistan, because I have come across them there, and of course all through the Near and Middle East. I believe that they are in Muslim Africa from something I have heard, but I will only speak from my own personal experience. I have met Naqshbandi Dervishes in Syria, in Damascus and in Aleppo. I have met them in Asia Minor. They may be distinguished from most of the Dervish Orders by certain striking characteristics. First of all, it is a principle of the Naqshbandi Order of Dervishes that man should aim at a complete harmony between his inner and outer life, and therefore they do not allow their own followers to withdraw in any way from the world. Wherever I have met Naqshbandi Dervishes, they have always been people engaged in the ordinary vocations of life—some rich, some poor, some learned, some very simple people, but always living an ordinary life; marrying, having children if it suits them, and prospering in the world, and also there is the very strong principle of mutual love and brotherhood which requires that they not only help other members of the same order but that they should always work for the good of their fellowmen round them. You will certainly recognize that all this corresponds to what Gurdjieff called the "Fourth Way."

The Naqshbandi Dervishes also—I may say this right away because I have seen this for myself —have considerable knowledge of techniques connected with the transformation of energy. There is, however, one very peculiar feature that I found it hard to fathom, and that is that one can never get any Naqshbandi Sheikh to tell you what is behind him; on the contrary, he will either tell you outright, or give you to understand, that he is the centre of their work. His pupils will assure you that he is the one Great Teacher and that there is no other. That is even when one knows that perhaps a mile or two away on the other side of a hill, there is another Naqshbandi Sheikh who is also regarded as the one and only teacher by his followers—as I have seen with my own eyes. One might think, well they are a funny lot, if the Naqshbandi Sheikhs all put themselves up as the one and only. There are only two places where I have come across Naqshbandis where I was told that there was a teacher beyond. That was once in Cehan and once in Istanbul. Always the finger was pointing towards the East. In each case I was told of a particular town. I was even told how, if I was prepared to do it, I could find my way to the <u>Mutessarif-i-Zeman</u> or Teacher of the Time. But I am pretty confident that even if I had found him there would still have remained a certain mystery; and one is inclined to ask oneself whether the Naqshbandi Order is really a prodigious secret society, hiding its organization very successfully by this device of appearing, wherever you touch it, to be at the centre, or whether in the nature of their work, and of their approach to the problem of life, there is this considerable degree of autonomy among the Sheikhs, or leaders or teachers. I think it is the latter. I think that the Naqshbandi Order is not an hierarchical one in the sense that there is a chain of authority. I think that it is quite true that they are more or less independent. Here again we have a characteristic feature of Fourth Way Schools as described by Gurdjieff. They are not 'permanent' or 'fixed;' but appear and disappear according to the needs of time and place. Nevertheless, Gurdjieff insisted that there is always an 'Inner Circle' accessible only to those who are able to serve its needs and tasks.

Now Gurdjieff was very emphatic when he spoke to us about all this. He said that the real place to go to is Bokhara. "If you really want to know the secrets of Islam," he said, "you will find them in Bokhara." This is equivalent to saying you will find them if you can find the centre of the Naqshbandi. It seemed clear enough from what he had said about this that these are the people who know about the Enneagram and who therefore have some very profound and extraordinary teachings.

I can point to another piece of evidence that confirms this interpretation, and this is to be found in the etymology of the word, Naqshband. The Order was founded in the fourteenth century by Muhammad

Bahauddin who died in A.D. 1390. The Order is not so very ancient compared with the Mevlevis who are contemporaries of the Franciscans or the Kadiris who are nearly as old as the Benedictines. What made Bahauddin assume the surname Naqshband? The word Naqsh means a seal, or a symbol, or sign, and Naqshband means one who seals or makes a sign. The word Naqshband can also be understood to mean those who make symbols, those who have the power to create a symbolism. It seems probable that Gurdjieff, when he was travelling in those parts at the end of the last and the beginning of this century, succeeded in making contact with these people and that he did so. He gives various hints as to what happened. These are distributed round chapters of his books, some in the chapter called 'The Bokharian Dervish Hadji Asvatz Troov,' some in the chapter that I have already referred to in the Second Series called 'Prince Yuri Lubovedsky,' others again in the chapter called 'Professor Skridlow,' which is the last chapter that has been published. In this way, we reach the conclusion that the knowledge that Gurdjieff afterwards taught as his 'Ideas' came from putting together two halves of a single truth. One half is found in the Western—chiefly Platonic—tradition and the other half is in the Eastern—chiefly Naqshband—tradition. This fusion of two halves is strongly hinted by Gurdjieff in the story of Boolmarshano in Chapter 44 of Beelzebub.

If this is right, then it means that at some fairly early date—before the coming of Christianity—there existed a great knowledge of the construction of the natural order and that this knowledge divided in some way; part of it coming to the West—almost certainly through Pythagoras as Plato suggests in the

Timaeus—and partly remaining in the East among the Chaldean Magi and moving up Northward when there was the break-up of the Achimenean Empire after Alexander's invasion. Some things that Gurdjieff spoke about, as when he said, "This that I am telling you now is very old, 4,500 years old," one may judge to be hyperbolical, but I believe it was most likely that he was in fact referring to the start of all this, when the Sumerian culture passed over into the beginning of what subsequently became the Chaldean culture. Probably very much more had been understood at that time about laws and the nature of man than we at present would be ready to believe. You may think that it is scarcely credible that things should be known by these "primitive" people, but if you actually see what they accomplished, you will not regard them as so primitive. If you look also at Egypt alongside and you ask yourself, "What was the relationship between the Sumerians and the Egyptians at the beginning of the third millenium B.C.?" then you may come to the conclusion that a very great deal was known at that time. Maybe we stand on their shoulders with all our modern science to a greater extent than we realize. We imagine that we—in the last three or four hundred years—have discovered practically everything that matters, just from nothing; from the ignorant astrologers and alchemists and the arbitrary and artificial speculations of the neo-Platonists.

Probably behind all this, there was a good deal more real knowledge about man and about the world than we are yet ready to admit.

Gurdjieff was certainly convinced of this, and he did, in his searching, set himself to unearth as much as he could. I have spoken to you this evening, mainly about his searchings in Central Asia, but I know that he also went down to Ethiopia and that he went very much further East. From the way he spoke he must have known the Pacific Islands—certainly the Solomon Islands, from having personally visited them. When he went to the Solomon Islands, he went in search of something, and there is something to be found there even now.

Let me now try to put all this a little bit together. His great good fortune, or fate, was that he was able to reach a source of really important traditional knowledge which may, according to my guess, somehow be connected with the Naqshbandi Dervishes. He also was able to find extremely practical and powerful methods for man to produce and control the fine substances that are connected with our psychic and spiritual experiences. He also did reach—chiefly, I suppose, by his own determined investigations—a very deep knowledge of the human psyche, rather different, and in some ways much more penetrating than that which Western psychology has found over the last sixty years.

Looking back now over some 43 years since I first came in contact with Gurdjieff, I am astonished to see how many of the things that then seemed outrageous contradictions of what was currently accepted by science and psychology have now come to be accepted. This is only in part due to Gurdjieff's own influence—but mainly because of the actual progress of these sciences themselves. It is striking, and I could give you a number of examples of things that seemed to us really strange when we heard them in 1921 or 22. For example, about the nature of extra-galactic space, the countless galaxies outside our galaxy. I cannot remember exactly when this was beginning to be accepted—but it was already strange to us then. It has now become commonplace.

Next week I am going to speak about the problem of deciding whether all that Gurdjieff produced was simply the result of his own researches, very cleverly put together by the concerted efforts of a group of quite outstanding men, or whether there is something more that cannot wholly be reduced to terms of a prodigious research into tradition and of an almost equally prodigious effort of synthesis. I have told you the story as far as I can tonight. Next week I am going to speak more about his actual teaching and methods from the time that he began to teach to the end of his life. I shall also say what I believe he really intended should come out of· his work.

QUESTIONS

Q. I am Armenian myself, but I am not familiar with the Armenian secret societies you referred to....

J.G.B. At least you are familiar with the Dashnak?

Q. That was a political party.

J.G.B. Much more than that.

Q. But not on the Mystical side?

J.G.B. All that I can say is that I personally have been in contact with people in 1919 and I am sure that there was also a mystical element in it. It appears on one side as a political party as I said. I had that real evidence about this from the Caucasus, there was also a religious and even mystical element.

Q. But the Dashnak is a political party founded with Marxism, and this is hardly mystical.

J.G.B. It only became a political party long after the time I am speaking of. In 1920 it was still a secret society. I can only tell you about people that I personally met when I was in Istanbul in 1919 and 1920. These people who were members of the Dashnak then were certainly not Marxists, that I can tell you for reasons that are quite categorical. The outward aim of the Dashnak was to secure the independence of Armenia. It was an Armenian nationalist movement, not political in the sense of being either Marxist or anti-Marxist at least at that time. I am perfectly confident that if you go back to the 1890's, when such societies already existed, that then they were simply to defend the Armenian way of life.

      Of course, it is perfectly true that they were a thorn in the flesh of the Tzarist Russian government of that time. But why? Because they wanted the independence of Armenia; they were also a thorn in the flesh for the Turkish government for the same reason. But this was only one side of it. What I do know from what Gurdjieff himself said about it, this part at least is verifiable——that the possibility that he had of travelling through what is now Armenia, and through Kurdistan, arose through his connection with one or other of these societies.

Q. Is anything known about his stay in India?

J.G.B. Very little. Only one, no doubt, totally apocryphal story of his own, that he met Madame Blavatsky when he was a boy of 17 or 18, and that Madame Blavatsky fell in love with him.

• • •

Q. Has the Enneagram definite characteristics? Is it a symbol of a society similar to the Pentagram? Has it any connection with others?

J.G.B. Very probably it is the emblem of a society. I am not now concerned with the interpretation, but I will certainly have something to say about it next week. I am only talking at the moment about its being a symbol, or Naqsh, that may be connected with a society, rather than with its being an instrument. The only time that I have heard of this apart from Gurdjieff's own reference as to its connection with the Bokharian Dervishes, is that somewhere in North India it is still used as an instrument for divination.

• • •

Q. Could you say something about the techniques for transforming energy?

J.G.B. All the part concerned with how he taught and what he taught I am reserving for the third lecture. Tonight I have been trying to indicate what appeared to be the probable sources and how he came to the material that he subsequently called his 'Ideas' or his 'System.' Of course, I shall have to speak about the transformation of energy next time to complete this very cursory presentation of the enigma of Gurdjieff. But you understand that I am not giving lectures on Gurdjieff's teaching so much as trying to show something about the strangeness of this man. Many, many people have travelled in these parts of the world, and nobody seems to have found the things that he found. At one time, I and many others, thought that it was something that he got from Western Traditions, and no doubt there have been Russian occultist societies that made an immensely diligent search of the material which fascinated many Russians at the end of the 19th century and the beginning of this century. It was only when we began to make a serious study of this in 1924, that we came to the conclusion that this was certainly not the explanation, that Gurdjieff must have found something quite different from what was available in Europe, and also quite apart from anything that was available in India—for it is not like the Tantric, or Buddhic, or what are known as the Theosophical sources. I have not spoken about all that tonight because that is mainly negative; but there are certain points of contact. Undoubtedly Gurdjieff has studied Buddhism quite seriously because there are certain features of Buddhist psychology that he has adopted and weaved into his own ideas. But these sort of more fundamental notions are not to be found, so far as I am aware, either in any of the classical Hindu philosophies or in the Tantra, or in Buddhism.

GURDJIEFF'S TEACHING AND METHODS

A striking characteristic of Gurdjieff's teaching and methods is that he never stood still. To the very end of his life he was experimenting and there was no stationary period, so far as I have been able to make out, from the time he began his active searches at the age of about 16, that is, about 1888, right up to the end of his life, in October 1949.

Experimentation can lead to misunderstanding because people acquainted with one particular period of his life may take it as being representative of the whole; and find themselves in complete contradiction with people who know a different period of his life. This also concerns statements which he made at one time, which might be thrown aside and contradicted thirty years or even thirty days later. Most of the books that have been written about Gurdjieff refer to particular periods of his life and therefore one cannot get an adequate picture from reading books alone.

There is one other characteristic of Gurdjieff that I must refer to at once; and that is, his adoption of a deliberate disguise in the form of putting himself in a bad light. He put on a mask that would tend to put people off, rather than draw them towards him. Now, this method—which is called by the Sufis, the <u>Way of Malamat</u>, or the method of Blame

—was highly esteemed in old times among the Sufis, who regarded the Sheikhs or Pirs who went by the Way of Blame, as particularly eminent in spirituality. Such people represented themselves to the outside world under a bad light, partly in order to avoid attracting praise and admiration towards themselves, and also partly as a personal protection. This way of Malamat has been lost to sight in modern times. It was certainly followed under other names in Christianity also and in all the great ways of religion. The attraction to oneself of blame rather than praise, has always been approved: but it is not very much understood at our present time, nor is it usually thought right to do so by deliberately performing blameworthy actions.

There is a particular reason for following the Way of Malamat, connected with the powers that surround people destined for a high eminence in the world or in spirituality. In the old Zoroastrian teaching, there was recognition of a certain power called Hvareno. This was a mark of kingship, and whoever had Hvareno had the power of attraction over people. He had the 'royal touch.' The same power was recognizable by certain marks or features of the physical body. These marks showed a man destined for a very high advancement which could either be material or spiritual. For example, the Buddha was said to bear such marks; which were recognized, when he was still a child. They showed that he was destined for a very high degree of spiritual advancement. It was not possible to tell whether this meant that he would become a great king destined to rule the world or that he would become a great spiritual Initiate. If a man bearing those marks, or having the power called Hvareno, wished to follow the way of spirituality, then he had to protect himself against being drawn into Messiahship, or the outward exaltation of his person. One reason for following the Way of Malamat, among people of very high spiritual destiny, is to protect themselves against being put upon a throne, as it were, and either served, or even worshipped.

The Gospels make it clear that Jesus had this Hvareno to a superlative degree so much so that the Jews wanted to take him by force and make him King. But we are told that each time this was threatened he withdrew and hid himself. This may be taken to mean that Jesus also followed the Way of Malamat expressed in the words, "He was despised and rejected of men." You may remember that in the Imitation of Christ, St. Thomas a Kempis advises Christians who wish to follow Christ to seek blame rather than praise in all that they do.

We may conclude then that the Way of Blame can belong to the very highest summit of spirituality since even Jesus Christ adopted it in order to fulfil His Mission upon earth. It seems even that it is right for everyone who is in danger of attracting to himself the wrong kind of hero-worship that verges on idolatry. The power of personal attraction is a terrible temptation that few can resist.

Gurdjieff realized at an early age that he did possess powers of this kind. I am not suggesting that Gurdjieff should be compared with Solomon or the Buddha, who are known to have these marks, but simply that he had a certain inborn quality of Hvareno and that he became aware that this quality could result in his coming to a position of external authority. He explains, in the writing to which I referred last week, <u>The Herald of Coming Good</u>, which he wrote in 1933, that twenty-one years earlier (that is, in 1912) he decided to adopt what he calls 'an unnatural way of living,' precisely in order to protect himself against the consequences of his own Hvareno.

A man who adopts that particular procedure is very hard to understand in terms of his external behaviour, and this has obviously been the case with Gurdjieff. People have tended to form judgments about him in terms of his outward behaviour, and have failed to take into account the possibility that this outward behaviour was deliberately adopted for the very purpose of which I am speaking now. He himself referred to this in <u>The Herald of Coming Good</u>; but soon after the publication of this book he suppressed it and withdrew as far as possible all copies from circulation, and probably comparatively few of you have come across it. This also was connected with the same need to disguise his real nature. He decided upon a course of action other than what was foreshadowed at the time that he published this book. This book was a <u>ballon d'essai</u> sent up to ascertain the consequences of announcing to the world that certain things were possible. And when he found that the consequences were such that there would be a serious misunderstanding of what he was attempting to do, he drew back and began to follow a more hidden way.

I think I can assure you from all my studies of his life and my various contacts with him that he really was a man who deliberately chose to hide his own powers behind behaviour that would attract blame. If you reflect on this you will see how very difficult it must be for us to disentangle from the outward show who was the real man and what were his real purposes. Before speaking about these, I must run briefly through the phases of his life during the period of his search; that is, from the age of about fifteen until his death. There were, first, the comparatively local searches and contacts made in that extraordinary region of the Caucasus, the meeting-point of Europe and Asia, where he was born and brought up. Then later, from about the middle 90's until early in the 20th century, he travelled very much more widely. And during this time also, there is no doubt, he spent considerable time in contact with a certain Brotherhood to which he refers a number of times, and where he learnt about an ancient and hidden tradition. This gave a new direction to his subsequent activities. After this period of searching, he entered upon a period of experimentation with the problem he had set himself; of finding a way to deliver mankind from the particular defect in human nature which, as he saw it, was going to be of increasing significance with the way the world was going. That feature of human nature is suggestibility; that is, the weakness of people in front of external suggestion, the tendency to follow the crowd and to be carried away by any kind of propaganda. With the advancing techniques of communication, this has become at the present time a very serious menace to the world. One result of suggestibility, when methods of communication develop, is that personal initiative tends to be stifled, and it becomes possible to control men's minds by suggestion to an extent that can become quite disastrous both to those who submit to control and also to those who exercise it. Aldous Huxley has drawn a picture in <u>Brave New World</u> of the limits to which this could go.

In order to study the problem of human suggestibility, Gurdjieff made profound investigations into hypnotism. In fact, the very first conversation I had with him, in 1920 on the first day I met him was about hypnotism. He then told me such astonishing things that I realized he had far deeper knowledge than anyone I had met. It so happened that in 1920, I was very much interested in this subject. Not only had I read a good deal about hypnotism, but I had also been instructed in it by an expert in the subject and had practised myself in order to see how far it could help me to understand certain conclusions connected with time and eternity which I had reached from mathematical studies. I spoke, therefore, with a certain experience; but it quickly became clear to me that I was a mere infant in the field of hypnotism compared with Gurdjieff. And not only I, but other people who had studied this rather deeply, whom I had personally met, such as Charles Lancelin, the well-known French occultist, were far from understanding what hypnotism could do for man.

Gurdjieff was engaged in the practical study of hypnotism between 1900 and 1908 and, as I said to you last week, he probably worked at this mainly in connection with the curing of people from alcoholism and addiction to opium, and also with various other influences that increase suggestibility and diminish the power of initiative in people.* During

---

* The main source of information about this is <u>The Herald of Coming Good</u>.

those years, Gurdjieff was trying to see whether he could establish a practical means for helping people with this grave human problem. I do not want to imply that suggestibility is the very centre of all man's troubles, because it is a derivative weakness that results from man's own egoism. If it were not for his egoism, he would not be suggestible. Nevertheless, suggestibility is a symptom and a manifestation of weakness that is more serious than most people nowadays are prepared to admit. We hear, of course, of things like brain-washing and propaganda for advertising and political purposes; but, in reality, this vice or weakness of suggestibility is deeper than these and the effect upon the human race will be disastrous unless it is counteracted.

Therefore, when Gurdjieff took as the theme of his study to discover means whereby mankind could be delivered from this psychic weakness, he was concerned with something that is really important for us all. Now, you cannot cure a symptom unless you can do something about the root cause from which this symptom comes. Behind suggestibility, there is a woeful ignorance of human nature, which is one of the awkwardnesses of our present situation. It is awkward just now because we know so very much about external nature, and so very little about internal nature, and this produces a rather threatening imbalance of our activity. We can work so effectively on the outside and remain ineffectual on the inside.

Gurdjieff was thus led to take a deep concern in man's own nature in order to find why people do not know themselves. It is probable that it was in this contact that he made with this particular

school of which I was speaking last week, he hit
upon the real explanation of this; which is very sel-
dom grasped nowadays, even, for example, by people
who have studied Gurdjieff's ideas either in writing
or even in practical ways. The basic illusion concerns the nature of consciousness. What we ordinarily call consciousness is only a reflection of consciousness. The true consciousness is the reverse
of what men call consciousness. Behind our ordinary
consciousness, there is another consciousness, but
it is more true to say that what we call consciousness, our ordinary consciousness, is, as it were,
a reversal of consciousness, rather like the negative
of a photograph where light seems dark and dark
seems light.

I think that when Gurdjieff came to understand this characteristic of our consciousness, he
then was able to see how his earlier studies of hypnotism really could be fitted into a more complete
picture of the human problem. In other words, it
was necessary to discover ways by which man could
enter into his true consciousness without, of course,
losing his contact with the external world, for which
we use our reversed consciousness, or, as it is often
called, rather misleadingly, lower consciousness.

Side by side with these discoveries about
human nature, there is no doubt that Gurdjieff was
also deeply interested in what he calls the Laws of
World Creation and World Maintenance, a name he
used to describe the knowledge for which man has
always searched that will enable him to understand
the world and his place in it. It is the need to learn
how the world is constructed and how it works, and
why it is that we men are able to be related to our

world in the way we are. This is a question that can hardly even be formulated by natural science which studies only that which can be known and not the source of knowledge itself, that is, man's own nature. Science accepts as a given fact that there is a being such as man in the midst of a world governed by laws of physical and chemical and biological processes, about which science cannot answer nor even ask. For that, it is necessary to have a total picture of the world in which man and his experience and the world and its nature are all brought together. It is the need to understand this total situation of man in relation to his total world that drove Gurdjieff towards anything that he could hear about in the nature of fundamental laws or principles and he came across some extraordinary knowledge in this field and was able between 1908 and 1912 to piece together a cosmology that he was never able to complete.

That brings us now to the fifth period of his life, that began about 1910, when Gurdjieff set himself—probably in collaboration with people who had joined him in his searches—to put all this material together; that is, to combine what he had learnt in psychology, in a practical way, particularly in his studies of hypnotism, with what he had learnt about laws and the structure of the world—that is cosmology. And so began to take shape what was later called 'Gurdjieff's System,' but which he himself usually called his Ideas. How long that period of synthetic activity lasted is difficult to say; because in a sense it was still in progress at the beginning of the First World War. By that time he had realized that, in order to make this synthesis, it was necessary to have people upon whom he could experiment. He set himself to found, first of all small groups of people here and there, and later what he called his Institute for the Harmonious Development of Man. He was no doubt connected with very exalted circles right up to the Tzar and his Court. He met Tzar Nicholas II a number of times. He spoke to us of his admiration and compassion for the Tzar and of the strange situation that existed round the Russian Court. As I think you know, his wife was a noble Polish lady from the Imperial Court.

That period, when Gurdjieff moved in rather high circles in Russia, leads up to the beginning of the 1914 war. It is very likely that, as he told us, he was in direct contact with Rasputin, the monk who had such a strange influence over the Russian Court and which Gurdjieff tried to counteract. Afterwards he rather withdrew from all that. Then came another period from 1915 on when Gurdjieff had met Ouspensky and the people that Ouspensky brought to him. During this time he had several experimental groups with which he worked through the war-years from 1915 until the revolution, when he withdrew to the Caucasus. His father was killed in the over-running of Kars by the Turks on 25th April 1918. It happens that we seem to know a good deal about Gurdjieff's activities during the period from 1915-1919 because of what Ouspensky has written in his book, In Search of the Miraculous. We must not forget that Ouspensky was in contact only with a small part of Gurdjieff's work. A number of the experiments that Gurdjieff started were cast aside and he began to work in different ways, so that what he did later represents an entirely new phase.

Now, you may ask, what was he experimenting with? Here I must say something about the very difficult problem of transferring <u>Understanding</u> from one environment to another. There is no doubt that in Asia there is a traditional wisdom of very great importance to mankind. Contrary to what is usually supposed, this is probably more highly developed in what is called the Middle East than in India and the Far East. But it does not really matter where it comes from, the point is that the transferring of this wisdom to our European environment is an exceedingly difficult matter; far more difficult than people suppose. There have been various premature attempts at bringing to the West notions and methods that have come from India, from China, from Japan, from the Middle East—from Buddhist, Hindu, Tantric, Zen, Sufi and other sources. Really serious difficulties have arisen, because those who have made the attempt to bring this wisdom to the West have either been Europeans who had imperfectly assimilated what the East had to give, or Asiatics who did not understand the European and American environment. In nearly every case they made serious mistakes, either in attempting to transfer exactly what worked extremely well under certain Asiatic conditions into quite different conditions, or in adapting it to the West without really having understood the new environment.

One of the chief tasks that Gurdjieff set himself to accomplish was to see how what he had found —particularly in Asia and to a minor extent in Africa —could be made available in a practical way to Western people. It took him something like thirty years of constant experimenting before he arrived at a method that he found reasonably satisfactory; and this in spite of the fact that he started with two considerable advantages. One was that he was, after all, himself of European origin, and the other, that his particular study had been of the defects in human nature that required to be overcome. His studies had not been directed solely to the perfecting of man—for example, by such methods as the direct penetration into the deeper consciousness by meditation—but he had studied deeply the obstacles in our nature that prevent us from living normal lives. This certainly gave him a considerable advantage when he came in contact with Western people because these obstacles are not so very different in East and West. The real difference between the East and West are more in the kind of things that we believe in and the kind of things that they believe in; the kind of things we hope for and the kind of things they hope for. That is why it is difficult for us to understand one another. It is not so much that our natures are different, but rather that we put our trust in things which they would not dream of trusting, and on the other hand they put their trust in things that we would not dream of trusting.

The task Gurdjieff set himself from about 1910, until about the early 1930's, corresponds to that period which I spoke of, when he said that for twenty-one years he set himself to live an unnatural life. Then, for a short time, he began to live normally again, and then afterwards he returned to a way of living difficult to understand.

I must say something now about the final outcome of all this, because I will not have time to speak at any greater length about the stages of his experimenting. You must remember what I said last week about substances, how in the Eastern countries —especially in the Middle East— more is understood about the substances that are behind activities, than we yet understand in the West. Gurdjieff was very clear about the importance for man of being able to produce and control the substances he requires in order to produce changes. He understood that you cannot improve the way something works if you continue to feed it with unsuitable fuel. You have to produce a more refined fuel to get a more refined action.

In connection with substances, there is little doubt that Gurdjieff, somewhere at the beginning of this century, came across a notion which he afterwards wrote about in the chapter called 'War,' of Beelzebub, where he refers to the learned Kurd Atarnakh, who discovered that the reason for war on earth lies not in the behaviour of human beings, but in the necessity for a particular substance which can only be produced in one of two ways; either by the conscious and intentional activity of people, or by their death. It follows that if people will not produce this substance intentionally, then deaths - and especially premature deaths—have to be increased on the earth. War becomes inevitable on this account. This notion implies that wars are the consequences of man's failure to perform his cosmic duties, and on account of this failure, conditions arise that make war inevitable. Or if not war, the premature dying of people has to be brought about. Since, according to this theory, the required substance is liberated by some kind of death, the result can presumably be obtained by an enormous increase in the world's population such as has occurred during the present century. This is hinted at by Gurdjieff at the end of Chapter XLIII of <u>Beelzebub</u>, when he refers to wolves, rats and mice. You are also no doubt aware of the suggestion that this process is somehow connected with 'feeding the moon.'

Whether we take these suggestions literally or figuratively, there is no doubt that Gurdjieff felt that he had come across a truth deeply significant for us all; namely, that man must either perform a certain duty for which he exists on the earth, or else be compelled to live and die in such a way that the results will be obtained from him willy-nilly, in spite of himself.

This notion can be put very simply in this way, that intentional actions, performed for a rightful end, result in a certain substance being released. One part of that substance goes into the performance of the action; one part of the energy becomes available for this purpose, whatever it is; and the third part of the energy becomes available for the perfection, the inner development and spiritualization of the person himself. Human life should be so organized that this transformation of energy is really consciously undertaken by a sufficient number of people, and only in that way can the hazards of human life be averted.*

This belief, in a slightly different garb, is not unfamiliar in the West in the doctrine of vicarious suffering and the transfer of merits. Gurdjieff regarded it as vital that men should recognize this duty and set themselves to work in such a way that

---

* For more details, read <u>Beelzebub</u>, pp. 1105-8.

it will be performed. In that way alone can a great danger to mankind be averted. Gurdjieff was concerned to set up conditions in which people could be shown, if they were willing to do it, how this transformation of substances can be undertaken; in other words, how man can perform his cosmic duty. The principle is that, in performing that duty, he both serves his fellow-men and also saves his own soul.

It so happens that this is intimately connected with the problem of suggestibility. A great deal turns upon people understanding that, if they are to perform their cosmic duty, they must liberate themselves from suggestibility. They must be independent and free people; who can freely and consciously assume and accept the duties they have to perform. So it comes to this, that it is necessary to show people how they can free themselves from the illusions and weaknesses that make them suggestible and self-indulgent, and also they must be shown how they can perform the task which is required of man. Of course, this latter can be shown in the form of moral codes, or the teaching and the practice of religion. These collectively constitute what is called the Ways of Objective Morality. Anyone who sincerely and wholeheartedly follows the practice of his or her religion and keeps to its commandments will produce the very same results as come from the conscious transformation of substances. Their way of living will give what can otherwise be obtained only by dying. Nevertheless, there is both a possibility and a need for a limited number of people to follow what are called the Ways of Accelerated Completion. These ways take different forms: some are connected with religion and others are not, but they all have in common the need for a more exactly and more personally regulated work of transformation than is possible by following rules or commandments formulated for the guidance of all and therefore of necessity very general and often vague. Among the Ways of Accelerated Completion is one called the <u>Fourth</u> <u>Way</u> which is characterized by the fulfilment of all ordinary life obligations, coupled with a very exactly regulated and very intensive personal work.

It will be obvious to anyone who has read Gurdjieff's writings and has some knowledge of his life that his interest was wholly concentrated upon the Fourth Way. This requires the highest degree of intelligence, adaptability and inner freedom in those who direct it; for they have to create conditions that enable the Duty of Transformation to be performed without neglect of the obligations common to all men and women. This brings us to the simple, practical question: what are the conditions that make it possible for man to fulfil his cosmic duty? For those who do not know of the Fourth Way it must appear that it is best done in retirement from life. The intensification and acceleration of this work was formerly supposed to be the task of monks and recluses, withdrawn from the world, who could devote the whole of their time and energy to this action which brings about the transformation of substances. It is probably true that this was more generally the case in earlier times, when the conditions of life on the earth were much simpler than they are now. But our present-day problem is different, and Gurdjieff was well aware that there is a far more intimate interlocking of lives on the earth, due to the progress of communications and various other technological advances; so that it is no longer possible to rely mainly upon withdrawal from the world in order to produce the required results. Therefore, it is necessary that means should be found whereby people can increase this work in the ordinary conditions of life. And this is the so very remarkable thing about the present century, that a number of new movements have appeared in all different parts of the world, under different names, connected with all the great religions of the world, but in every case, there has been a movement towards the carrying out of one's spiritual obligations in the ordinary conditions of life.

You will perhaps conclude that all these movements belong to what I have called the Fourth Way. Unfortunately, there are many imitations of this way that entirely lack the quality of accelerated completion which is the only justification for departing from the Ways of Objective Morality. This is a very interesting thing, which I have myself studied, as well as I can. In perhaps twenty or thirty different movements I know of the one really common feature is that they do take as a principle that man can live a complete life, outwardly and inwardly, without withdrawing from the world, and without abandoning the ordinary responsibilities of man—to marry, to bear children, to accomplish certain external work in the world and so on. And yet it can by no means be said that they are all—or even the majority of them part of the Fourth Way. There is far too much theory and too little practice in many of these movements and in others there is a lack of flexibility in method that is quite incompatible with the demands of accelerated completion.

I am not concerned at the moment with the abortive attempts at establishing centres of Fourth Way work, but rather at the widespread recognition that such work is needed. I think that this is not merely a consequence of the changing outlook of the twentieth century, perhaps even the reverse, it may be that our outlook is changing just because this kind of new appreciation is entering. It is felt that people living ordinary lives must be able to make a contribution towards the solution of the great problems of mankind. And so it is that we see for example in the Christian Churches—how the division of priest and layman is diminishing everywhere. There is recognition of the importance of the religious and spiritual life of people who are not, as it were, specialists, i.e. priests; this is now admitted to a degree that would have been unthinkable a hundred years ago. The same is also true in Buddhism. It is much less than a hundred years ago that the only people who were regarded as seriously religious were the monks or Bhikkus. The lay Buddhist was content to live an ordinary life with no expectation of attaining anything, except possibly at some time, reincarnating under conditions that would enable him to withdraw from the world. The cannonical Buddhist books—the Pali Pitakas—are entirely orientated towards that notion of the complete, unquestionable superiority of life of the Bhikku, of the one who renounces the world, over the life of the ordinary worldly man. To an extraordinary degree, in this 20th century, Buddhism has abandoned this traditional attitude, and there are movements—such as the Satipatthena movement in Burma—which show the ordinary layman how to meditate in such a way that he can be given the expectation of attaining the spiritual development that was previously thought to be reserved to the Bhikku.

Having introduced the notion of the Fourth Way I must refer to another important feature, that, namely, it has no permanent form, no permanent place, no centre. It is constantly searching and adapting itself. It does so, not for the purpose of improving its own content, but for the purpose of performing a task. There is a certain Work to be done in the world, and in order to do that work some people must come to the requisite understanding. People who suffer from suggestibility, from weakness in relation to the external world, who do not know themselves—and especially those who remain in the ordinary reversed consciousness, or semi-consciousness—such people cannot effectively or directly perform this task, with its different specific undertakings. Therefore, it is necessary, for those who have responsibilities in this direction, to help people to prepare themselves if they choose and if they wish to do so.

This leads to a very important distinction. There is primarily this notion which belongs to the twentieth century, that spiritual development does not require, in our time, withdrawal from the responsibilities of life; that is, to make it one's professional job to be spiritual. That is the first thing which is common, as I say, and is permeating everything, both the known religious practices of man and also all kinds of new movements that have arisen. Secondly, and this is less clearly understood, is the notion that accelerated development is associated with the carrying out of certain <u>Work</u>. The notion of the Fourth Way is wholly bound up with these two principles; the first is that of complete involvement in life externally, and secondly, in the acceptance internally of responsibility for certain work that is required for a great Cosmic Purpose

According to Gurdjieff, this purpose is concerned with the transformation of substances whereby the destiny of mankind as a whole can be kept moving in the right way. This takes many forms. It can take the form of activities of artistic creation; it can take the form of certain kinds of social organizations; it can take the forms of the transmission of specialized forms of knowledge, or research into the conditions of mankind, and preparation for the future, and certain other tasks, more specifically connected with what I said; that is, the transformation of substances.

I am personally confident, from long years of study of this matter and having been in contact with a rather unusually large number of people who have been concerned in this particular field, that there really is such Work and that there are people who understand it in a way that is not obviously visible on the surface. This means that there is in effect a <u>Twofold Life</u> on the earth. One is the visible, external life in which we all have to participate, and the other is an invisible life in which we can participate if we choose. In a sense one can say the first life is a causal life; that is to say, in that life causes that exist in the past produce results that are being experienced in the present and which will be carried forward in the future. It can also be called the stream of happenings. It is of course called by such names of Samsara and the Wheel of Life, and so on, but in a very simple way it is the ordinary life that we all live. The second, the other life, is <u>non-causal</u>, which means that it exists only in so far as it is created. It is the life of <u>Creativity</u>. Every creative act rightly performed is a means of participation in that life. And the search for creation is the search for that life.

Creation is infinitely varied in its content and its forms. Everything that is going on everywhere is also a field of possible creativity, and therefore there is no limit to what can be found in the field of creation. But the great majority of mankind are content to live in the first life. A few are searching for the other, because there is a feeling of a need to participate in creative activity and a realization that one is only half alive, and perhaps not even that, if one is not participating.

This is what is meant by the word <u>Work</u>, and when we talk about 'the work' or the Great Work—<u>Magnum Opus</u>—it refers to the invisible world which has to be perpetually created in order that it should <u>be</u>. And it is that that we are called to if we are destined for accelerated completion. In order to enter that world, we have to earn the right to be in it, and for that we have to bring to it something <u>made by ourselves</u>. The first and simplest thing we can bring is our own capacity for work; our own capacity for transforming energy, and therefore for participating in the Creation. This can afterwards be converted into specific forms of creativity, according to objective needs and our own subjective powers.

There is no doubt that the Fourth Way is the direct application of the principle of creativity in life. That is why I called it <u>non-causal</u>. It always has to start without an antecedent cause. It is a spontaneous call from beyond that makes this possible. I am not going into this in detail. I would have to give a philosophical lecture, and I would be in danger of having to answer philosophical questions; but let me just say this simply, that there is a Work to be done, and that some people have the feeling that their life is not complete unless they are participating in that Work. It is to such people that these lectures are addressed.

Gurdjieff found a direct way of participating and he tried to bring this in such a form that it should be available to us, to people of our Western world. He certainly did not create this form, nor was he the founder of this way—but, I think there are probably certain things connected with this where Gurdjieff had a sort of special inspiration connected with the transition from the past to the new epoch into which mankind is now entering. What is significant about the future of our world is the coming unification of every form of human experience. The Work is concerned with bringing people together and not with separating them. I am sure that this is a very visible characteristic of this twentieth century of ours. In one way, this obligation to unite stirs up most serious reactions, and therefore we have seen troublesome wars and hostilities and hatreds. But if you look behind all this, you can see they all come about because there is an urge to unite and not to isolate. One very obvious feature of this is the increase in tolerance that has come over the world, and the mutual acceptance by people which is perhaps the most hopeful and admirable feature of our century, with all its depressing features.

Now, what does this add up to in practice for us, and what was Gurdjieff really after? There is a very interesting hint that he gives——I think it is not in any of the published writings about it——in certain lectures that he gave in New York in the early 1930's, and he refers to it very specifically in this book, I mentioned, The Herald of Coming Good. That is his hope that it would be possible to found on the earth, Clubs of a new kind. He took this extremely seriously, although he was never able to realize it during his life. He saw that it was necessary for people to be able to meet and to exchange experiences. But the way they do so under present circumstances is foolish because they usually exchange experiences and converse only about things that are trivial and external, or else they do so under highly formal and ritualistic conditions. Gurdjieff wanted to see the possibility for people to meet and share in experience so that many types of people would come in contact with one another, and that understanding of the problem of human life and the way in which people should live should spread. Right up to the end of his life, he used to speak about the gravity of the problem. In other words, what he wanted to do was by no means esoteric, or hidden; on the contrary, he was very much concerned that as many people as possible should realize that there is this problem of human life and that this realization should be shared and faced. He saw that it was inevitable there would be many different ways of interpreting and understanding this, and hoped that some means could be found by which there should be some kind of common ground on the basis of which people could meet. I think he had hoped, during

his lifetime, that he would be able to make a definite start towards this, but he was singularly unfortunate. His initial attempt in France, at Fontaine-
bleu, failed and just when he had really prepared
things again in the late 1930's, the Second World
War broke out. After the war, he was too ill and
too near the end of his life to be able to do much,
though he did make one very serious effort to found
a place outside Paris.

I think that Gurdjieff hoped that what he had
discovered and understood about these questions
would be freely spread among people, without any
sort of secrecy, and that people should be made to
realize that it is possible for anyone who is prepared to do so, to participate in the task of living
his or her life in such a way that it is productive in
the Creative World. For some people, this can be
carried very much further and they can attain what
Gurdjieff called 'accelerated results.' He certainly
believed that it is possible for other people, without
having the same intensity of living for themselves,
to participate in this general process. It is the obligation of those who have more strength in this field
to share with others, so that there can be a general
spreading of this understanding of the way of life
and the ability to live it. This is intimately connected with the transformation of substances. It
means, in simple language, that those who are spiritually strong can help those who are spiritually
weak——not by their outward actions alone but by
lending them a supply of the 'substance of work.'
It is somewhat analagous to the 'Queen Substance'
that the Queen Bee produces and that makes possible all the activity of the worker bees. This very

important notion was first explained to me by Gurdjieff in July 1923 and I have referred to it briefly in
my book, Witness (p. 116). If you can understand
this, you will have come near to the very essence of
the meaning of man's life on the earth. Gurdjieff
had the power to produce the 'substance of work' and
those of us who knew him were able to draw upon it.
But there are other and more powerful reserves of
this substance than any one man can produce.

So we come back again to the question of
where Gurdjieff himself stood in relation to the total
work proceeding on the earth. Much confusion has
arisen on account of Gurdjieff's own special way of
living personally that I referred to earlier as the Way
of Blame. People have been led to think that it was
necessary that the work should be repellant. I am
sure this was not Gurdjieff's intention. All that he
wanted to avoid—was that people should become
dependent upon him, that they should direct their
suggestibility towards him and turn to him as a kind
of leader-figure. His aim was that people should
become free. It was only for himself, personally,
that this particular method was applicable, and when
he saw anyone else imitating it, he turned on them
with the utmost ferocity and said,"This is quite unnecessary for you and stupidity that you should do
this yourself." In other words, if people who were
connected with him, began to imitate his rather in-
comprehensible behaviour and attract blame towards
themselves he was quite merciless in pointing out
that this was quite unnecessary for them and therefore totally wrong. It was only necessary for him
because of the peculiar task which he had set himself.

He certainly was under some special kind of obligation, that in the particular work he had to do, he should not assume a position of being a great teacher, with a large number of pupils depending upon him. It was often very obvious that with the greatest of ease, if he had chosen to do so, he could have exercised the power he had to attract people. He could have had thousands of people round him, and he could have spread his methods, which are really extraordinarily valuable for people who wish to live their lives better among thousands of people instead of a relatively small number. But he deliberately abstained from anything of this sort for some reason which I think I know, but which it would not be right to speak about this time.

I have tried to give you some notion about this peculiar man and the way his work developed, and I think that it is much more important in relation to the whole human problem than most people realize; that is to say, Gurdjieff was making a very great effort to play his part, but it is not, by any means, the whole story. There is a whole process going on in the world just now; a whole creative activity concerned with lifting man over the present interval into a new cycle, so that this new cycle should be entered without too serious handicaps from the past. This is happening in so many ways, with such an intricate interworking, that as I grow older and see more and more of it—I happen to live in such a situation that I see it in many parts of the world—I am really in wonderment at the extraordinary power, the super-human intelligence and consciousness that is directing the hidden affairs of mankind at the present time.

My purpose in giving these lectures was not simply to chat about Gurdjieff; but also to tell you that there are certain directions in which I think it is now possible to carry forward this work in a very productive way.*

Editor's note: Mr. Bennett then referred to projects concerning his own current Work before finishing the lecture.

WORKS CITED

The following list provides the reader with information regarding related works mentioned within Mr. Bennett's lectures. Page numbers following the titles indicate where the reader may find these discussions.

Gurdjieff's Background

Gurdjieff, G. I., *Meetings with Remarkable Men,* pp. 10, 12, 18, 23, 24, 25

The Sources of Gurdjieff's Ideas

Bennett, J. G., *et al, Enneagram Studies* (for exposition), p. 49
Bohme, Jacob, *Aurora,* p. 46
Godwin, Joselyn, *Robert Fludd* (for his diagrams), p. 46
Gurdjieff, G. I., *Beelzebub's Tales,* pp. 33, 41, 48
_____ *The Boolmarshano* (pp. 1132 ff), p. 54
_____ *The Herald of Coming Good,* p. 36
_____ *Meetings with Remarkable Men,* pp. 30, 33
Hastings, James, *Encyclopedia of Religion and Ethics,* p. 35
Kepler, Johan, "Cosmographic Treatise," see de Lubicz, R.A., *Egyptian Miracle,* (pp. 151-163), p. 47
Plato, *Timeaus,* pp. 46, 55

Gurdjieff's Teaching and Methods

Gurdjieff, G. I., *Beelzebub's Tales,* for the following:
    Kurd Atarnakh, (*op cit.* pp. 1094-1104), p. 73
    Wolves, rats and mice, (p. 1116), p. 74
    Birth rate, (pp. 1105-1108), p. 74
_____ *The Herald of Coming Good,* pp. 64, 66

Huxley, Aldous, *Brave New World*, p. 66
Ouspensky, P. D., *In Search of the Miraculous*, p. 70
St. Thomas a Kempis, *Imitation of Christ*, p. 63